Published by YOUniversal Center Los Angeles, California

contact: info@youniversal.org

DANCING
INTO
THE LIGHT

AN INNER JOURNEY GUIDED BY
RUMI

TRANSLATIONS BY
OMID ARABIAN

ILLUSTRATIONS BY
SHILLA SHAKOORI

{ In Gratitude }

First and foremost, I offer gratitude to the spirit of Rumi, and to A.M.S. for opening my heart's eyes to this magnificent spirit.

This is the second collection of translations to come out of a course I have conducted since 2010, and so I am grateful to all who have attended and/or supported the course and shared their insights on these poems.

I am overjoyed that Shilla Shakoori has offered her marvelous drawings to illustrate this book, and I thank her sincerely for her kindness.

Always and forever I am indebted to Mojdeh for far more than can be enumerated here.

Last but by no means least, I offer gratitude to you, the reader, for taking this journey into the heart of all that is, with Rumi as your guide.

O.A.

POEMS

The poems that follow are selections from *Divan-e Shams-e Tabrizi* and *Masnavi*, the two major works of Jalaaleddin Mohammad Balkhi, known as Rumi (1207 - 1273 CE). The original source poem for each translation appears in the last section of the book, along with a corresponding transliteration.

While any act of translation inherently involves some degree of subjective interpretation, I have striven to keep as much as possible to the letter of Rumi's verses, not just to their spirit.

Readers are invited to delve into this collection with an open heart, and use Rumi's mystical poems as vehicles for their own inquiry into the great metaphysical questions of existence.

While the scope of each poem is by no means limited to one or two subjects, I have very loosely organized the selections in this volume by the following topics:

THE DIVINE HUMAN

{ 1 }

You are
an edition
of the divine book;
you are
a mirror,
reflecting the King's beauty.

Whatever is in this world
is not outside of you;
whatever you want,
seek it within yourself -
because you are it!

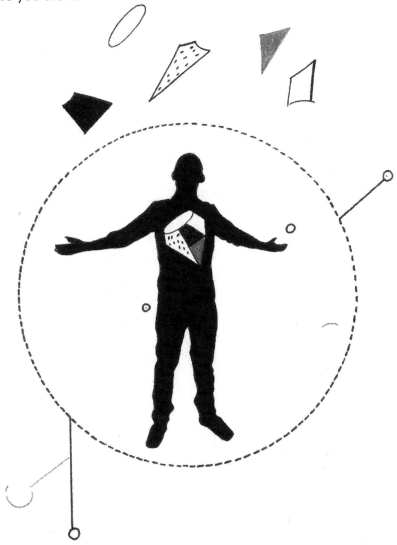

{ 2 }

You have the nature of God
when you enter into the heart:
the light of Mount Sinai
will radiate from within your chest.

You have the nature of light
when you enter a house at night:
the entire house will glow
from the brightness of that light.

You have the nature of wine
when you join any gathering:
from your beauty will arise
thousands of passions,
boundless fervor.

If joy has disappeared,
if desire has flown away,
when you let the water flow
oh, what flowers and plants will grow.

Even if the world is in sorrow,
if happiness has died away,
oh, what other worlds you can bring
from the unseen, into the seen.

This yearning within the restless
stems from you -
otherwise,
what could the dark mud know
of purity and clarity?

With one breath you weep
and with another, you till the soil -
but you are not a scavenger!
You are the mine,
you are the elixir.

{ Note: This is a segment of a longer poem. }

{ 3 }

We live
by the grace
of that glorious light;
strangers,
yet deeply familiar.

Our ego is like a wolf;
but in secret,
we are grander
than Joseph in Egypt.

The moon
will abandon her vanity
if we
show our face to her.

The sun
will set fire to her lofty feathers
if we
spread our feathers and wings.

This human body is but a robe -
we are
that to which everyone prays;
we are
that before which everything bows.

Set your sights on the breath,
not on the body;
and let your heart be stolen
delicately,
tenderly.

The devil
saw only divisions,
and imagined
that we are separate from Truth,
separate from God.

{ 3 cont. }

Even Shams of Tabriz*
is but a pretext -
we are it!
We are the virtuous,
we are grace itself.

Tell the masses, as a guise
that *'He is the noble king,
and we are but beggars.'*

What do we need
from kings and beggars?
Joyously, we belong
with the true King!

By virtue of Shams,
we've disappeared;
beyond appearances
there is no He
and there is no Us.

---

*Shamseddin of Tabriz - 'Shams' for short - was Rumi's master and, for many years, his inseparable companion. The word 'Shams', rooted in Arabic, means 'sun'.

SPIRIT

{ 4 }

There is a spirit
 - signless -
and we
are immersed in signs of it;
there is a spirit
 - placeless -
and yet
head to toe
is its place.

Do you want to find it?
Then don't seek it
for a moment!
Do you want to know?
Then don't know it
for a moment!

When you seek it
in the unseen,
you are far away
from its evident self;
and when you seek it
in the seen,
you are veiled
from its hidden self.

But when you step out
of hidden and evident,
when you step out
of logic and deduction,
you can stretch your legs
and rest, happily,
in her protection,
in peace.

When you relinquish the road
a spirit will start to spring forth;
and then,
oh what grace will flow
from her essence,
from her flowing spirit.

You
who have imprisoned the spirit:
how long
will you pull back the reins?
Charge ahead,
hurtle it forward -
but not into this world.

Come out of greed,
take envy, and render it blind;
then stamp your feet
and celebrate -
for envy and greed
cannot speak of her.

How long will you run,
like the lowly,
for two loaves of bread?
How long,
for three loaves of bread
will you endure the spears?

{ 5 }

The spirit is a vessel
that does what no other can:
it receives from the pure realm
and delivers unto the realm of soil.

Restlessly in love,
its work is to manifest;
it acquires from the heavenly throne
and pours onto the earth.

Once, it was not aware
of this realm, where it delivers -
if only it were aware, now,
of the realm where it receives!

From what spirits have bestowed
the land has become radiant
like a goldmine!
If only the soil had tongues
so it could speak of this...

So it could speak of the forest -
that eternal grove -
the one that feeds our spirit
secretly, invisibly...

In that forest
leopards and deer roar,
calling out to the divine -
to the one who tends to our sighs,
the one who draws us in.

A lion who feeds our self
with her own milk -
a lion who liberates
our selves from our selves...

A lion
who appears to us as a deer -
and in that guise,
lures us into the forest.

{ 6 }

If you find
the scent of spirit
emanating
from the hidden Beloved
- if you catch just one glimpse -
you will not be contained
in a hundred worlds.

When you accept
the seal of spirit,
you'll be king
without an army;
you'll conquer
the hidden realm,
and know what is unseen.

That treasure you've heard about -
the one you've chosen to dream of -
if you haven't found it on earth
you will find it in the sky.

If you are a guardian of love,
you will find
so much beauty -
effortlessly seen,
effortlessly yours.

In that blessed mirror
- clear, pure, and free of doubt -
you will find,
one by one,
signs of paradise
here in this very world.

Piereced by love's arrow,
intoxicated by the Beloved,
you may lose this life -
but you'll find
a hundred other lives.

The key
to the most intricate spells
will be effortlessly yours -
if you find
a moment's respite
from your whims and desires.

Shatter all the idols
on behalf of the King of life -
until you find,
in plain sight,
the one who gave form
to them all.

O Tabriz:
through Shams
- that light of truth -
you will find,
beyond doubt,
countless revelations
hidden in absolute mystery.

ORIGIN, BIRTH, DEATH

{ 7 }

Long before
there were grapes
and vineyards in this world,
our essence
was intoxicated
with that eternal wine.

Long before
all this commotion,
long before
Mansur made his declaration*
and headed for the gallows,
at the center of the world of spirit
in the divine city
we would proclaim:
I am Truth.

Long before
the one who is the Self of all
began to build
in the world of water and soil,
our joyous feast was under way
in the unbuilt tavern of truths.

Our spirit was as the universe
its cup was as the sun;
and by the grace of its wine
the world was basked in light,
up to its neck.

O wine-giver,
take these lofty ones
- so enamored with their water and soil -
and render them drunk;
so each one will realize
what a treasure he's left unheeded.

I'll give my life to the wine-giver
who arrives by way of the heart
so she can lift the masks
from all that is unseen.

Our mouths are open
in yearning and wonder
before that wine-giver who brings
casks of the wine
that does not obscure,
honey without the bees.

O wine-giver:
close my mouth
or I will reveal
the treasure of the seventh realm -
the one that is
the source of all treasures!

City of Tabriz,
speak, if you know;
speak of that time
when Shamseddin was exalted
without having been Shamseddin.

{ continued }

---

*Mansur Al-Hallaj was a 9th-C. Persian mystic who declared, 'I am the Truth.' He was executed for heresy.

{ 8 }

I've come again, I've come again
I've come from the Beloved's side;
gaze onto me, gaze onto me --
I've come to shelter you from grief.

I've come in joy, completely free
from everyone and everything;
many thousands of years passed
before I could begin to speak.

I'm going there, I'm going there;
I was up high, so I ascend;
set me free, set me free again --
I've come transient to this terrain.

I was a bird of celestial air;
see how I took material form?
I didn't see her lure, and so,
swiftly I came, entwined in her.

I am the purest light, it's true;
and not a mere handful of soil;
I'm not the shell, for after all
I am the pearl, a royal gem.

Don't look at me with head-locked eyes;
look with your eyes of mystery;
come over there, then look at me -
for there I bear no heavy load.

I'm greater than the four mothers;
than seven fathers, greater still;
I was a jewel inside the mine,
I've come here to see and be seen.

My Beloved's come to market;
nimble and conscious, she has come --
why else would I have ventured here?
I've only come desiring her.

Shams of Tabriz, when will you gaze
upon the whole of creation?
For in this desert of decay
I've come to give my heart and soul.

{ 9 }

On the day of my death
as my coffin passes by,
do not imagine
that I ache for this world.

Do not weep for me,
and don't cry out
"Alas, alas" -
you will fall
into the demon's trap
and that is cause
for true regret.

When you see my corpse,
do not speak of separation -
to me, that is the time
for meeting, for union.

When you entrust me to the grave,
do not say
"Goodbye, goodbye" -
for the grave is simply a veil
obscuring the crowds
just on the other side.

When you see me descend,
look for me to ascend -
when the sun descends,
when the moon descends,
do they suffer, is it a loss?

It may seem like setting to you,
but it is an arising -
when the grave becomes a prison
the spirit becomes free.

When a seed penetrates the earth
does it not sprout out?
Why then, do you have doubts
about the human seed?

{ continued }

{ 9 cont. }

When a pail enters the well
does it not come out full?
Why, then, would the Joseph* of spirit
cry out in fear
when entering the well?

When you close your mouth
on this side,
you can open it on the other -
your true voice rings out
in the atmosphere of no-place.

It may seem to you
that I have been buried -
but in truth,
I dwell
above all the seven skies.

---

*Joseph, son of Jacob, is a biblical character who was cast into a well and left to die by his own envious brothers. He was extracted from the well only to be sold into slavery, but eventually became the savior of Egypt during a time of famine.

REALITY, ILLUSION, TRUTH

{ 10 }

A Sufi entered a garden
seeking freedom and expansion;
he set his head upon his knees
as Sufis are known to do...

As he sank deeply into himself,
a meddlesome one passed by
and became distressed
by the Sufi's seeming slumber.

"Why do you sleep," he said?
"Awake, and gaze at the vines!
Behold these trees,
all these beautiful greens!

Listen to the Lord's command:
turn towards His creation,
and witness the evidence
of His grace!"*

The Sufi replied:
"O frivolous one,
all signs of Him are in the heart!
And what is outside?
Signs of signs,
nothing more.

The gardens, the meadows
are all within the spirit;
their reflection
forms the outside world,
just as an image falls
upon running water.

What falls upon the water
is an illusory garden
undulating
as the pure water moves.

But the groves
and the fruits
are within the heart -
it is their reflection
that falls upon
this water and mud.

If this world were not
an image of that heavenly cypress,
then God would not have called it
the realm of deception.**

All the deceived
have gathered round this image,
believing
- in error -
that here is the true grove.

They run away
from the gardens' source
and live a life of absurdity
built upon an illusion.

When they awaken
from this sleep of ignorance
they will see the truth
but what will it serve them
then?

Blessed are the ones
who die before their death -
for they have caught a scent
of the true source
of this vineyard."

---

*A reference to the Qur'an, Surat-ar-Rum, verse 50.
**A reference to the Qur'an, Surat-al-Hadid, verse 20.

{ 11 }

Train your eyes on the wine-giver
and not on the one who drinks;
gaze upon Joseph
and not upon your hand.

You are life itself -
a fish in the net of body;
gaze upon the fisherman
and not upon the net.

Behold the essence
which you were at the start -
not the trifle
with which it is now adjoined.

Set your sights
on the endless meadow of flowers -
not on the thorn
scraping your foot.

Look at the regal bird
casting her shadow upon your head -
not at the crow
that leaps from your hand.

Grow upward
like the cypress and the hyacinth
and don't look down
like the violet does.

With the water of life
flowing in your channel,
don't look at the jug and the cask -
even if they break.

Grow towards the one
who gives life, and intoxicates -
don't moan about what is not
and don't focus on what is.

{ 11 cont. }

Look at contentment:
it is male, agile and spry -
don't gaze upon the female:
pregnant, and wanting.

See the ones who are pure
rising swiftly to the top -
don't gaze upon the residue
sinking to the bottom

Glimpse the heavenly faces
that fill the world,
and disregard the forms
that stand in your way.

In love's lure
there are strange and marvelous birds -
pay no heed the owl
who's abandoned the coop.

There is a hidden speaker
far more skilled than you;
so don't gaze upon the one
who is,
at this moment,
in silence.

{ 12 }

Visions of her are in your heart
so that you don't look here and there;
and she shows infinite grace
so that you won't come up
against any limits.

You'll take the seat of power
and dwell in abundance -
reside with Sufis of pure, vast vision -
if you set foot
outside this six-sided cloister.

You possess a door
- by nature invisible -
so don't search for doors
in the six directions;
a hidden door
through which you fly out
every night.

As you fly,
your feet are tethered
to an imaginary thread -
so that you don't fly out
once and for all -
so that at dawn,
you can be reeled back in ...

So that you will return
to this prison of a womb
until your creation is complete -
for this world is as a womb
and you are to be nurtured
by this blood.

When the spirit grows its wings
it will break through the body's egg;
it will fly out,
like the winged Ja'far*
and radiate its rays of gold.

---

*Ja'far ibn Abi Talib, a companion of Islam's prophet Mohammad, lost his arms in
battle and was said to have been awarded wings in their stead.

LOVE

{ 13 }

This time,
I've become
entirely entwined in love;
this time,
I've cut off altogether
from well-being and comfort.

I have detached from myself -
now something else
keeps me alive;
I've set fire at the root
to my thoughts,
to my mind,
to my desiring heart.

O everyone, o everyone,
I cannot be like all the rest!
What I've envisioned
in my heart
would not cross
even a lunatic's mind!

The lunatic has shed his tears
and run away
from the passion I feel -
I've mingled
with the magnificent
and flown
in the realm of non-being.

Today, my mind
has altogether abandoned me -
it keeps trying to frighten me,
imagining that I can't see!

But why should I
be frightened by the mind?
It's for the mind's sake
that I have taken form!
Why should I be confused?
I have bewildered the one
who tries to bewilder me!

There's a purpose
for which I have stayed
in this prison of a world -
why else would I be imprisoned?
I am not a thief!

In the body's prison
I am immersed in blood;
it is for the sake of the unruly ones
that I have streaked my garment
with blood,
with soil.

Like a baby in the womb
I am being nurtured by blood!
Humans are born only once -
but I have been born
so many times!

You are drunk and light-headed -
I am drunk and joyous
without a head!
You are smiling and in love -
I am laughing
without a mouth!

I am that rare bird
who's left the garden
and leapt into this cage
- eagerly, willingly -
without a trap,
without a trapper

For this cage,
in the company of friends,
is far more joyous
than any garden,
than any field.
It is for the sake of the Josephs*
that I reside
within this well.

*See p. 34.

{ 14 }

Once again,
love pours forth
from my walls,
from my door;
once again,
my vengeful camel
has broken free from its binds.

Once again,
the lion of love
spreads its blood-streaked claws;
once again
my rabid heart
is thirsty for blood.

Once again
the new moon has arrived -
it's time for insanity!
All my knowledge
- alas -
how useless it has been!

Once again,
rebellion is born,
and a new army is formed;
once again
my sleepless Beloved
has severed me from sleep.

My dreams
have left me impatient,
my mind
has been washed away;
the Beloved
has lightened my load,
relieved me of my work -
now what is my task?

Rise up,
rise up again -
the uprising has arrived!
My fire, my passion,
fuels a hundred uprisings!

If Autumn has burned the garden,
like a lover's heart,
now my Beloved's face
is my garden, my meadow.

The worldly garden is scorched,
and the heart's garden
is illuminated;
this world's mysteries are burnt,
and my mysteries
are revealed.

O my caged body,
it's time to rejoice!
O my ailing heart,
the gift of wellness has arrived!

O wine-giver,
keeper of the tavern:
go and pawn my robes
- everything that I own -
in gratitude
for this gift.

{ 15 }

Look and see
love
mingled with lovers;
look and see
the spirit
mingled with the dustbowl.

How long will you see
this and that,
good and bad?
Look and see, at last,
this and that
mingled together.

How long will you speak
of seen and unseen?
Look and see
the unseen
mingled with the seen.

How long will you speak
of this world and that world?
Look and see
that world
mingled with this world.

The heart is as the king:
it speaks,
and the tongue translates;
look and see
the king
mingled with the translator.

Come and mingle -
for it is for our sake
that the earth
has mingled with the heavens.

Look and see
water and fire,
earth and wind -
enemies, mingled as friends.

{ continued }

Wolf and ram,
lion and deer,
these adversaries
mingled together
in deference to the master.

Though they are tricksters and foes,
yet,
like bow and arrow
they are co-mingled.

Look and see
a King
by whose grace
flowers and thorns
mingle in the meadow.

Look and see
a cloud
by whose bounty
water from so many gutters
has intermingled.

Look and see
oneness
in its evidence,
and know
that Spring and Autumn
are joined together.

Fill your mouth with sugar
and fall silent;
find it a shame
for sugar and advice
to mingle in your mouth.

Shams of Tabriz
emanates from the heart;
there is no-one
as mingled
as he.

{ 16 }

How astounding,
when the sun enters Aries
in Autumn!
My blood has come to a boil
and dances in the body's rivers
a glorious dance!

Look upon this dance:
the waves of blood;
look upon the fields:
teeming with lunatics;
look and see
this unconditional joy
immune to the sword of time.

Corpses come to life;
old age becomes youth;
bronze becomes gold
while still in the mine -
in our city
everything transforms
for the better.

A city brimming with love
and elation;
every drunkard
holding a grand cup
in every direction,
raising a toast;
here, a river of milk
there, a river of honey!

Cities have one king,
but this strange city
is filled with kings!
The sky has one Moon,
but this sky
is filled with Moons, and Saturns.

Go,
go and tell the doctors:
you have no work there -
for in that place
there is no disease,
no-one can be harmed,
no disorder can be found.

No judges,
no policemen,
no ruler,
and no constables -
no-one keeping tabs.
How can conflict,
enmity,
and war
exist
upon the waters of the sea?

{ 17 }

For those who travel the path,
the mind is a chain -
break the chain,
and the way is clear.

The mind is a chain,
the heart's desires a deceit,
and this life a veil;
the path is hidden
behind these three.

When you rise up -
out of mind,
out of heart,
out of this life -
certainty arrives
amidst uncertainty.

A man is not a man
unless he's gone beyond himself -
love without pain
is but a fairy tale.

Make your chest a target
for the Beloved's arrows -
always in the bow
and ready to fly.

The heart that is stung
by her arrows
will have
a hundred targets in its sights.

Love is not
for the faint and the meek -
love is the work
of heroes and warriors.

Those who serve lovers
rule the world,
and hold all its fortune.

{ continued }

Don't ask people about love -
ask Love!
Love is a cloud
that rains down pearls.

It does not need me to explain -
love is its own explanation.

If you are headed
for the seventh sky,
Love is the proper ladder.

Wherever there's a caravan,
traveling,
it goes toward love.

This world
sparks out of you -
don't let it lure you away
from love.

Now close your mouth,
like a shell,
and fall silent;
for your tongue
is your mortal enemy.

Shams of Tabriz arrived
and life is filled with joy -
for he is one
with that eternal Sun.

YEARNING

{ 18 }

Show your face -
I crave
meadows and gardens;
part your lips -
I crave
abundant sugar.

Light of virtue,
come out for a moment
from behind the clouds -
I crave
that radiant, glowing face.

I heard, once again,
the sound of drums
coming from your direction -
and so I returned
craving the King's embrace.

Coyly you said,
"Go, disturb me no more!"
I yearn to hear your voice
telling me again to go.

Bread and water
in this world
is like a flash-flood:
faithless, untrue;
I am a fish, I am a whale -
I crave the gulf,
the ocean's mouth.

This city, without you,
is a prison I swear -
I yearn to roam
in the mountains, in the deserts.

I am tired
of flimsy friends
and meek companions -
I yearn to be
with the warriors,
the lions of God.

{ continued }

{ 18 cont. }

My soul
is weighed down
by the Pharaoh
and his tyranny -
I yearn to see
the shining face of Moses.

I am weary
of these weeping mobs
and their complaints -
I yearn
for uproar
and drunken howls!

One hand holding a cup of wine,
one hand caressing my Beloved's hair -
I yearn to dance
at the circle's center!

I can sing
better than a nightingale -
but because of these jealous hordes
my lips are sealed
while, all along,
I yearn to burst out in song.

Long ago,
a sage circled the town*
holding a lantern;
"I am tired
of these beasts and brutes!"
he said -
"I seek
a human being."

"We have all looked," they said,
"but none could be found."
"That's what I yearn for,"
he replied -
"the one who cannot be found."

---

*A reference to Diogenes of Sinope, the Greek philosopher who was often seen
carrying a lantern in daylight, searching for an honest man.

{ 19 }

I am ecstatic,
yet I want
to be more so;
I gaze into your drunken eyes
and say,
this is how I want to be.

I don't want a crown,
I don't want a throne;
I want to be
fallen on the ground
at your service.

My Beloved
took me by the throat
and said,
"What do you want?"
This, I answered –
just this, is what I want.

I want to breathe
the divine air;
but,
as I have my own breath,
I seek a grand companion -
a glorious confidant.

I am in the circle:
entering into the divine presence,
sheltered from all calamity;
I am as wax
searching for your ring,
yearning for your seal.

There is a different moon
hidden
in the heart of this moon;
I know this to be true, in fact,
but I want the certainty
that comes through vision.

{ 20 }

My task
is no task at all!
I am in love,
and in your love
there is no disgrace.

I've been captured
by the lion of your yearning;
and now, that lion
is my only prey.

What a rare pearl you are
within this ocean:
rendering me restless
like a wave.

I reside
at your ocean's shore;
drunk from your lips
though I have no-one to embrace.

I comfort my belly
with your wine -
the wine that leaves
no hunger, and no thirst.

Your wine
arrives for me from the sky,
and so
I don't have to beg and plead
with every common wine-maker.

Your wine
won't let mountains stay still -
so don't deride
if I've lost my dignity,
my gravity.

I conquer the world
like light from the sun -
without an army,
without a single horse.

{ continued }

{ 20 cont. }

And though I have no master
- no patron in this world -
neither am I weighed down
by useless woes and headaches.

So let me reside
along your street -
for there is nowhere else
for me to be.

Like sugar,
I've mingled with your rose;
it's no wonder then
that I am free of all thorns!

You are the axis of the universe -
everything faces you!
And so I will only
revolve around you.

My family
are those who are born of love;
for me
there is no more joyous tribe.

What is greater than both worlds?
The City of Love!
There is no better city for me;
no better land.

If I never write another word
after this,
it is not because
I don't have a beauty
to write about.

HOPING, TRUSTING, ALLOWING

{ 21 }

Do not lose hope,
never despair -
for if today
the Beloved drives you away,
don't you know
that tomorrow
she will call you to herself?

If she closes the door to you
don't run away;
remain, patiently -
for on the other side of patience
she will seat you
at the highest seat.

And even if
she shuts all the roads
and all the passageways,
she'll show you
a hidden passage
unseen by anyone.

When a butcher
cuts off the ram's head
he doesn't discard his kill -
but picks it up
and carries it on his shoulder...

And when the ram's breath
is all gone
he fills it up
with his own breath.*
Oh,
where will the divine breath
take you?
You will see,
you will see...

I say this only to illustrate;
but in truth, her grace
does not bring death to anyone -
but rather,
rescues all from death.

She'll grant Solomon's kingdom
to an ant;
she'll gift both worlds
and never turn away a heart.

My heart circled
round the world
and found
not a single one like her!
Who is she like?
Who is she like?
Who is she like?
Who is she like?

Silence -
for without words,
she will bring
a taste of this wine
- a taste of this wine -
to everyone.

---

*Inflating the animal's carcass allowed for easier removal of the hide. Rumi cites this ritual symbolically, to suggest re-animation through divine love.

{ 22 }

My sweet Beloved
shows no bitterness;
she never leaves my mouth
empty of wine.

Every dawn
she disrobes me -
"Approach," she says
"and I'll remove your cloak."

She surges into my house,
leaving me no respite;
she never ceases,
so how could I?

Her wine
has left my head spinning;
visions of her
have rendered my body
nothing but spirit.

Seven heavens
cannot contain her
and yet ... how does she travel
contained in my garments?

Feeding on her nectar
I am lion-hearted;
when she roars
I speak sweet words.

"You are in my grasp," she says
"I've created you -
you are my instrument
and so I shall play you,
caress you."

"I am your lyre," I say
"and when you strike me,
when you strum
each one of my veins,
I will yield, I will yield."

In short,
you will never
banish me from your heart;
and me -
I've lost my heart -
now what shall I do?

{ 23 }

Little by little
the league of drunkards arrives;
little by little
the wine-worshippers arrive.

Softly, gently
the ones who caress the heart
are on their way;
beautiful as flowers
they arrive
from the meadow.

Little by little
from this world of *is* and *is not*
those who are not, leave;
and those who are, arrive.

Skirtfuls of gold,
each as vast as a mine,
arrive for the poor,
for those in need.

The weary and gaunt
return from love's pasture
healthy and stout.

The essence of the pure
like rays of the sun
arrives from high above
shining down.

Joyous is that garden
where, in the depth of winter,
fresh fruits arrive
for the holy mothers.

They are, in essence, grace
and the reflection of grace;
from one meadow to another
they arrive.

{ 24 }

Every moment
of each day
a new thought
enters your chest
like a dear guest.

A sorrowful thought
may steal away happiness,
but also serves it.

By sweeping the house
of what does not belong,
it makes way
for a new happiness
to appear from the source.

It shakes off
the yellow leaves
from the heart's branches
so green leaves can grow
in their stead.

It uproots old cheer
so new passion can enter
splendidly
from the beyond.

Sorrow weeds out
old, rotten roots
so new roots,
yet unseen,
can appear.

Whatever sorrow purges,
or takes out from the heart,
in its stead it brings
something better indeed.

This is true especially
for those who are certain of it -
for sorrow is the servant
of those who dwell in trust.

If clouds and lightning
don't bring the sky to a frown,
the plants will die
of too many smiles from the
sun.

Each time
a new thought
enters your chest,
go to greet it
with a smile,
with a laugh.

{ 25 }

Humans devise, and plot, and scheme
unaware of divine will -
but plotting and scheming
is nothing like divine will.

When the human thinks with his mind,
it's obvious what he'll envision;
he'll plot and scheme,
not knowing how to be God.

He'll take a step or two forward
as though he's going the right way;
but then, who knows
where he might be pulled!

Let go of the quarrel
and seek the Kingdom of Love -
for that kingdom will liberate you
from the angel of death.

Become a quarry unto the King,
and seek less your own prey -
for whatever you hunt
the hawk of time will take back.

Fall silent, and choose a place
where you will be at peace -
for whatever place you choose
the King will seat you there.

{ 26 }

Who would write on something
that has been written upon?
Or plant a young tree
where another already grows?

She'll seek paper
that has not been marked;
she'll sow seeds
upon lands unsown.

You my brother,
be an unplanted field;
be a white sheet of paper,
unwritten upon...

So that your greatness
can be written upon you;
so that the divine
can plant seeds in you.

PURPOSE & ACTION

{ 27 }

Rise up, rise up,
for we are fellow warriors -
besides love,
besides love,
we have no other task,
no other mission.

In this soil, in this soil,
in this immaculate field,
we sow the seeds of love -
only love,
only kindness -
and nothing else.

How drunk we are,
how intoxicated
from that King who is us!
Come, come, let us get to work.

What did we drink?
What did we drink, that long-ago night,
that today, we are unquenchable drinkers -
always intoxicated,
and always wanting more!

Don't ask us, don't ask us
about the state of truth;
for we are wine-worshippers -
we do not count the cups!

You are not yet drunk -
you haven't feasted on that wine;
what do you know,
what do you know
of our hunt? of our prey?

We will not rest upon this soil
dormant and prone,
like so much straw!
We shall rise above this wheel -
for we are warriors
surrounding our foes.

{ 28 }

How long
will you hold back
that laughter -
that glorious, dazzling moon?

Your true face
will make servants
of a hundred kings;
your laughter
will turn servants
into kings.

Teach the crimson rose
to laugh...
unveil
that eternal wealth.

The gates of the sky are shut
only to attract
a conqueror like you!

Trains of drunken camels
are watching,
waiting,
for someone to steer them!

Let down your hair,
and lure a hundred thieves
into your locks,
into the circle.

The day of union is here
and the Beloved is ready, present -
so don't even glance at the future.

The hard-faced drum
loves to be struck;
the reed
is yearning to be kissed,
dreaming...

{ continued }

{ 28 cont. }

So strike
the drum's face
and give breath
to the reed.

And if the lyre begins
to beckon and moan,
open your hand,
and caress it
generously.

If this poem remains imperfect,
don't deride -
my mind is unruly
and thoughts are fleeting.

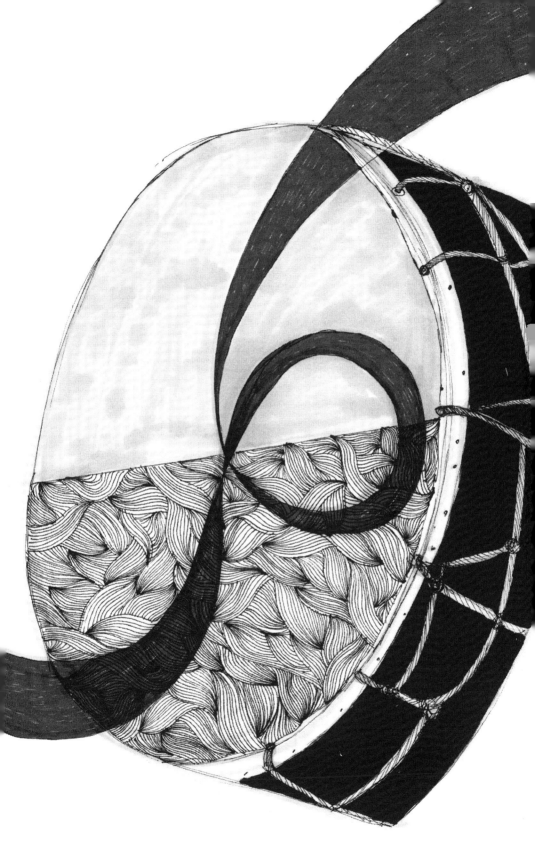

{ 29 }

I set a new fire
to my being,
and entered
a new non-being,
a new void.

Good and bad exist
in the world of existence -
but I am not good, brother,
nor am I bad.

Like the night watchman
I prowled
and reclaimed
from the thieving wheel
what it had taken from me.

I was a solitary one
with a hundred pompous selves;
now,
the solitary one is gone
– no trace of it left -
and I am a hundred -
I am the all.

One cannot come this way
without surpassing the self;
I left that self behind,
then came on my way.

My stature was dwarfed
by the stature of Love;
when my grandness became vile,
then I became grand.

I learned from the divine
the craft of being human;
now I am Love's champion,
joined with the divine.

Twenty-nine letters
on the tablet of life;
I've cleared off all the letters,
all the words,
and gone back to the start.

Shams of Tabriz
shone like a star,
and in his presence
my fortune, too, is bright.

JOY

{ 30 }

I have made a pact with joy
for joy to be forever mine;
I've made a pledge
with Life of Life
for her to remain my Beloved.

The great Ruler
has given me a decree
written by her own hand:
that she shall be the one I serve
for as long as there's a throne.

Whether I am sober
or completely drunk,
no-one else W
will take my hand and guide;
and if I should injure my hand
she will be my healer, too.

Idle thoughts do not dare
circle around my city walls -
who can transgress my borders
while she is my emperor?

By the grace of her ruby lips
my face is never pale;
even Rostam* will fall before me
for she is my warrior.

I will strike fear in Venus
and graze the face of the moon;
I will conquer the heavens
for she is my Saturn.

I illuminate the world
as long as I receive the sun;
I rule the mallet and the ball
when the heart is my arena.

I am Egypt, immersed in sugar
holding Joseph** in my arms -
what land of plenty do I seek?
She is my promised land!

Guardian,
keeper,
liberator...
she is ever-present
and self-evident proof
for me
and for all who deny.

There is a spirit in the world
that shuns all form -
and yet,
she takes human shape
and becomes
my humanity.

---

*Rostam is the foremost hero of Ferdowsi's epic poem *Shahnameh* (10th C. CE).
**See p. 34

{ 31 }

O lovers,
every moment
a toast:
to your joyous revelries -
may you turn this world
into a sugar mine!

O lovers,
your drunken dance
has reached the great throne;
this lovers' caravan
has left the earth
and surpassed the heavens.

O lovers,
how can I speak
of the ocean's shore,
when the ocean of life
has no shores at all!
It is greater than place
and greater than no-place.

O lovers,
like waves we rise up,
and bow down in worship -
so that the unseen
can become seen.

O lovers,
if someone asks,
who are you warriors
answer them thus:
we are the life
of life
of life.

O lovers,
the ocean of life
is giving and generous -
always gifting priceless gems
even to those
who are not divers.

{ continued }

{ 31 cont. }

O lovers,
with this event
and that event
the masses were swindled -
but we became free
once again
from this and from that.

O lovers,
beneath my feet
there are flowers,
and beneath theirs
there is mud -
this is how I dance
and stomp my feet
among the deniers,
surrounded by cynics.

O lovers,
how blissful, that moment
when
drunk with the beloved,
our spirit does not know
up from down,
this from that.

O lovers,
this ocean of love
is a wonder indeed
neither below
nor above
and not in between -
but suspended
and afloat.

O lovers,
when rays of Shams
appear from the East,
heaven and earth become
nothing but spirit...
pure,
free,
untethered spirit.

{ 32 }

I am a servant of the Moon -
so speak only of the Moon!
Speak to me of candlelight,
of sweetness,
and of nothing else.

Speak not of suffering,
only of treasure -
and if this is not known to you,
suffer not,
and speak not.

Last night,
as I roared in madness,
Love saw me, and said:
I'm here,
no need to wail
or tear your garments -
just say nothing.

I said:
O love,
there is something else I fear.

Love said:
That something else
does not exist -
say no more.

I will whisper in your ear
mysterious words;
just nod your head
in consent,
and beyond that gesture
say no more.

On the heart's journey
upon love's path,
a beauty came into view -
as though life itself
had appeared...
Oh how sweet this journey!
How exquisite!

I asked my heart:
Who is this beauty?
My heart replied
with a gesture:
It's beyond your grasp,
greater than you can fathom -
so say nothing, and travel on.

Awestruck, I asked,
Is it an angel's face?
Or a human being's?

Hush, replied my heart,
it is beyond human,
and beyond angel.

What is it then?
Tell me, I begged,
I am in a frenzy!

Stay in this state,
my heart replied,
and say nothing.

You dwell in a house
of fantasies and illusion!
Arise,
pack your bags,
leave this house,
and say no more.

O heart, I said,
speak as a father would -
is this not a tale of God?

Yes,
my heart replied,
but swear on your father's life
that you will say no more!

UNION

{ 33 }

With each breath
love's call arrives
from every direction,
left and right;
we are headed for the sky
but who is going to see whom?

We've resided in the sky,
companions of angels;
once again, we journey there
for that is our native land.

We are higher than the sky,
we are greater than angels -
then why not surpass them both?
Our home is the divine throne!

What is the world of soil
compared to the pure essence?
Where have you landed?
What is this place?
Pack your bags!

New fortune is on our side;
our task is to give our life;
divine light,
the pride of the universe
is leading our caravan.

This gentle breeze
bears the scent of her locks;
my brilliant visions
emanate
from her dazzling face.

Look into this heart of ours:
every moment, a miracle!
In spite of this spectacle,
your eyes are looking elsewhere -
why?

Humans are like water-fowl:
born from the ocean of life -
why would a bird make its nest
here
when it has arisen from that sea?

No, we are in the ocean,
all of us present within her -
if not, then why
do waves continually arise
from the ocean of the heart?

Now.
that primordial wave has come,
headed for this vessel,
this body,
this ship;
once again,
when the ship is shattered,
it's time for union
face to face.

{ 34 }

It's time for union,
face-to-face;
it's time for uprising,
for immortality;
it's time for tenderness
and benevolence;
the sea of light
is luminous and undimmed.

A royal decree has appeared
proclaiming abundance,
urging generosity;
the ocean's roar
can be heard;
good fortune has dawned,
but it is not merely morning -
it is the light of the divine.

What are these images?
Whose are these faces?
Who is this King, this ruler,
this ancient consciousness?
There are so many veils!

The cure for the veils
is upheavals like this!
The wellspring of these waters
is in your head, is in your eyes.

Twist around in your head,
but know
that you have two heads:
an earthly one,
made of soil,
and a pure one,
from the heavens.

So many pure heads
have fallen to the ground
so that you may know
that this head exists
by virtue of the other head.

The true, essential head is hidden,
and this minor one evident;
but know,
that behind this world
is another, infinite realm.

Now lid the cask
o water-bearer,
our water-jugs can take no more -
our perceptions are constricted
living in this constricted world.

Out from Tabriz shone Shams
- the Light of Truth -
and to him I said:
your light is joined
with everyone,
and at the same time
singular.

{ 35 }

With each breath, love's call arrives
from every direction, left and right;
we are headed for the fields,
but who is going to see whom?

The time for houses has passed –
the time for meadows is here;
prosperity has dawned, and now
it's time for union, face to face.

O blessed king, arise, arise,
awake from your heavy sleep;
ride, ride upon fortune's horse –
it's time for us to conjoin.

Hear the drums, recall your oath;
the way to the sky is swept clean;
your joy is the currency –
no sign of tomorrow's debts.

Light has lifted up its hands,
and shattered the dark of night;
the whole world, above and below
is full of clarity and radiance.

How blissful are the ones unbound
by these colors and these scents –
for there are, beyond all this,
so many colors in the heart.

How blessed that heart, that spirit
who becomes free from water and mud –
though within this water and mud
lies the means for alchemy.

{ 36 }

Sprinkle water upon the road* -
the Beloved arrives!
Bring the garden this good news:
the scent of Spring arrives!

Clear the way for her -
that enchanting full moon;
for it's from her dazzling face
that our light arrives.

The sky is torn asunder;
there's a rumbling in the world;
the scent of ambergris and musk is in the air;
the Beloved's banner arrives.

The splendor of the garden arrives;
the eyes, and the light of the eyes, arrives;
sorrow steps aside,
and beauty arrives at our side.

The arrows fly effortlessly
and sail towards the target -
then why are we sitting back?
The King arrives at the hunt!

The garden salutes,
and the cypress rises up;
the blades of grass march ahead,
and the flowerbuds arrive
riding on their stems.

The sky-dwellers drink and drink
until the spirit is intoxicated,
and even the intellect arrives
thirsty for wine.

As you arrive in our realm, know
that silence is our nature -
for it's when we chatter on
that dust and grime arrives.

---

*A reference to the practice of dampening the dirt road that led to a house, to
prevent dust from rising around honored guests as they arrived.

{ 37 }

Now I've seen you
in your wholeness,
and so, from here on
I will not become
fragmented,
distressed;
I've seen your path,
and so, from here on
I will not travel the path
of these others.

You,
who are the king of this garden:
you feed and nurture
me, and countless more;
you satiate
my eyes, and my heart -
and so,
I will no longer be a fool
for this meager table.

Now,
Ka'beh* has come to me
and so
I will no longer travel to Ka'beh;
my moon
has come down to earth -
and so,
I will no longer aim for Saturn.

I am stout, and proud
by virtue of you;
I am bound to you,
and free by virtue of you;
I will no longer be bound
by the devil.

You rule
space and time,
hidden and evident,
like knowingness;
you are life
and the universe itself -
in your presence,
why would I not become
all spirit,
fully alive?

---

*Ka'beh - a small cube-shaped building in Mecca (Saudi Arabia) - is the focal point of
the Islamic ritual pilgrimage called Hajj, and regarded by many as the house of God.

{ Originals & Transliterations }

In the pages that follow you will find Rumi's original Farsi poems, which correspond by number to the preceding translations.

For those who do not read Farsi but wish to hear what the original verses sound like, there is also a transliteration of each poem on the facing page. A key to the transliterations is below.

farsi letter/sound	transliteration	as in (english word)
اَ	a	cat
آ	aa	car
اُ	o	for
او	oo	book
اِ	e	bed
ی	ee	sleep
ی	i	big
چ	ch	chalk
خ	kh	khutzpah
ژ	zh	measure
ق / غ	qh	qanat
گ	g	good

In addition, a capital H is used to denote a hard 'h' sound
in the middle or at the end of a word, as in 'mohair'.

{ 1 }

ey noskheh-ye naameh-ye elaahi keh toyee
vey aayeneh-ye jamaal-e shaahi keh toyee

biroon ze-to neest har cheh dar aalam hast
dar khod betalab har-aancheh khaahi keh toyee

{ ۱ }

ای نسخه‌ی نامه‌ی الهی که توئی
وی آینه‌ی جمال شاهی که توئی

بیرون ز تو نیست هرچه در عالم هست
در خود بطلب هر آنچه خواهی که توئی

{ 2 }

sefat-e khodaay daari cho beh sineh-ii daraayi
lama'aan-e toor-e seenaa to ze seeneh vaa-namaayi

sefat-e cheraaqh daari cho beh khaaneh shab daraayi
hameh khaaneh noor geerad ze forooqh-e rowshanaayi

sefat-e sharaab daari to beh majlesi keh baashi
do-hezaar shoor-o fetneh fekani ze khosh-laqhaayi

cho tarab rameedeh baashad, cho havas pareedeh baashad
cheh giaah-o-gol berooyad cho to khosh koni saqhaayi

cho jahaan fesordeh baashad, cho neshaat mordeh baashad
che jahaan-haaye digar keh ze qheyb bargoshaayi

ze to-ast in taqhaazaa be daroon-e bee-qharaaraan
va agar na teereh gel raa be safaa che aashenaayi?

nafasi sereshk reezi, nafasi to khaak beezi
na qhoraazeh-jooyi aakhar, hameh kaan-o kimiyaayi

صفت خدای داری چو به سینه‌ای درآیی
لمعان طور سینا تو ز سینه وانمایی

صفت چراغ داری چو به خانه شب درآیی
همه خانه نور گیرد ز فروغ روشنایی

صفت شراب داری تو به مجلسی که باشی
دو هزار شور و فتنه فکنی ز خوش لقایی

چو طرب رمیده باشد چو هوس پریده باشد
چه گیاه و گل بروید چو تو خوش کنی سقایی

چو جهان فسرده باشد چو نشاط مرده باشد
چه جهان‌های دیگر که ز غیب برگشایی

ز تو است این تقاضا به درون بی‌قراران
و اگر نه تیره گل را به صفا چه آشنایی

نفسی سرشک ریزی نفسی تو خاک بیزی
نه قراضه جویی آخر همه کان و کیمیایی

{ 3 }

maa zendeh beh noor-e kebriyaayeem
beegaaneh vo sakht aashenaayeem

nafsast cho gorg, leek dar ser
bar yoosof-e mesr bar-fazaayeem

maH towbeh konad ze kheesh-beenee
gar maa rokh-e khod beh-maH namaayeem

dar-soozad parr-o baal khorsheed
chon maa par-o baal bargoshaayeem

in heykal-e aadam-ast roopoosh
maa qhebleh-ye jomleh sojdeh-haayeem

aan dam benegar, mabin to aadam
taa jaant beh lotf dar-robaayeem

eblees nazar jodaa-jodaa daasht
pendaasht keh maa ze-haqh joddaayeem

shams-e tabreez khod bahaanast
maayeem, beh hosen-e lotf, maayeem

baa khalqh begoo baraa-ye roopoosh
koo shaaH-e kareem-o maa gedaayeem

maa raa cheh zeh shaahHi-o gedaayi?
shaadeem keh shaah raa sezaayeem

maHveem beh hosn-e shams-e tabriz
dar maHv nah 'oo bovad, nah maayeem!

{ ۳ }

ما زنده به نور کبریاییم
بیگانه و سخت آشناییم

نفس است چو گرگ لیک در سر
بر یوسف مصر برفزاییم

مه توبه کند ز خویش بینی
گر ما رخ خود به مه نماییم

درسوزد پر و بال خورشید
چون ما پر و بال برگشاییم

این هیکل آدم است روپوش
ما قبله ی جمله سجده هاییم

آن دم بنگر مبین تو آدم
تا جانت به لطف دررباییم

ابلیس نظر جدا جدا داشت
پنداشت که ما ز حق جداییم

شمس تبریز خود بهانه است
ماییم به حسن لطف ماییم

با خلق بگو برای روپوش
کاو شاه کریم و ما گداییم

ما را چه ز شاهی و گدایی
شادیم که شاه را سزاییم

محویم به حسن شمس تبریز
در محو نه او بود نه ماییم

{ 4 }

rooheest bee-neshaan-o, maa qharqheh dar neshaanash
rooheest bee-makaan-o, sar taa qhadam makaanash

khaahi keh taa biyaabi? yek lahzeh-ii majooyash
khaahi keh taa bedaani? yek lahzeh-ii madaanash

chon dar nahaansh jooyi, doori ze-aashkaarash
chon aashekaar jooyi, mahjoobi az nahaanash

chon z'aashkaar-o penhaan biroon shodi-yo borhaan
paahaa deraaz kon khosh, mikhosb dar amaanash

chon to ze raH bemaani, jaani ravaaneh gardad
vaangaH cheh raHmat aayad az jaan-o az ravaanash

ey habs kardeh jaan raa, taa kay keshi anaan raa?
dartaaz, dar-jahaanash, ammaa na dar jahaanash

bi herss koob paayi, az koori-ye hasad raa
ziraa hasad nagooyad az herss tarjomaanash

aakhar ze-baHr-e doe naan, taa kay davi cho doonan?
vaakhar ze baHr-e seh naan, taa kay khori senaanash?

روحیست بی‌نشان و ما غرقه در نشانش
روحیست بی‌مکان و سر تا قدم مکانش

خواهی که تا بیابی یك لحظه‌ای مجویش
خواهی که تا بدانی یك لحظه‌ای مدانش

چون در نهانش جویی دوری ز آشکارش
چون آشکار جویی محجوبی از نهانش

چون ز آشکار و پنهان بیرون شدی و برهان
پاها دراز کن خوش می‌خسب در امانش

چون تو ز ره بمانی جانی روانه گردد
وانگه چه رحمت آید از جان و از روانش

ای حبس کرده جان را تا کی کشی عنان را
درتاز درجهانش اما نه در جهانش

بی‌حرص کوب پایی از کوری حسد را
زیرا حسد نگوید از حرص ترجمانش

آخر ز بهر دو نان تا کی چو دونان
و آخر ز بهر سه نان تا کی خوری سنانش

{ 5 }

peymaaneh-iist in jaan, peymaaneh in cheh daanad?
az paak meepazeerad, dar khaak meeresaanad

dar eshqh-e bee-qharaarash, benmoodanast kaarash
az arsh meesetaanad, bar farsh meefeshaanad

baari nabood aagaH zin soo keh meeresaanad
ey kaash aagaHasti zaan soo keh meesetaanad

khaak az nesaar-e jaanhaa taabaan shodeh cho kaanhaa
koo khaak raa zabaanhaa taa nokteh-ii jahaanad

taa dam zanad ze beesheh, zaan beesheh-ye hameesheh
kaan beesheh jaan-e maa raa, penhaan cheh meecharaanad

aan jaa palang-o aahoo, na'areh zanaan keh yaahoo
ey aaH raa panaaH oo, maa raa keh meekeshaanad

sheeree keh kheesh-e maa raa, joz sheer-e kheesh nadhad
sheeree keh kheesh-e maa raa az kheesh meerahaanad

aan sheer kheesh bar maa jelveh konad cho aahoo
maa raa beh in farib oo, taa beesheh meedavaanad

پیمانه ای است این جان پیمانه این چه داند
از پاک میپذیرد در خاک میرساند

در عشق بیقرارش بنمودنست کارش
از عرش میستاند بر فرش میفشاند

باری نبود آگه زین سو که میرساند
ای کاش آگهستی زان سو که میستاند

خاک از نثار جانها تابان شده چو کانها
کو خاک را زبانها تا نکته ای جهاند

تا دم زند ز بیشه زآن بیشه ی همیشه
کان بیشه جان ما را پنهان چه میچراند

آنجا پلنگ و آهو نعره زنان که یا هو
ای آه را پناه او ما را که میکشاند

شیری که خویش ما را جز شیر خویش ندهد
شیری که خویش ما را از خویش میرهاند

آن شیر خویش بر ما جلوه کند چو آهو
ما را به این فریب او تا بیشه میدواند

{ 6 }

az delbar-e nahaani gar booye jaan biyaabi
dar sad jahaan nagonji gar yek neshaan biyaabi

chon moHr-e jaan pazeeri, bee lashkari ameeri
ham molk-e qheyb geeri, ham qheyb-daan biyaabi

ganji keh to sheneedi, sowdaa-ye aan gozeedi
gar dar zamin nadeedi, dar aasemaan biyaabi

dar eshqh agar ameeni, ey bas botaan-e cheeni
ham raayegaan bebeeni, ham raayegaan biyaabi

dar aayeney mobaarak, aan saaf-e saaf-e bee-shak
naqhsh-e behesht yak yak ham dar jahaan biyaabi

chon teer-e eshqh khastat, ma'ashooqh kard mastat
gar jaan beshod ze dastat, sad hamchonaan biyaabi

qhofl-e telesm-e moshkel saHlat shavad beh haasel
gar az vasaavas-e del hek dam amaan biyaabi

dar ham shekan botaan raa az baHr-e shaaH-e jaan raa
taa naqsh-band-e aan raa andar ayaan biyaabi

tabreez, dar mohaqhaqh, az shams-e mellat-o haqh
dar ramz-haaye motlaqh sad tarjomaan biyaabi

از دلبر نهانی گر بوی جان بیابی
در صد جهان نگنجی گر یك نشان بیابی

چون مهر جان پذیری بی‌لشکری امیری
هم ملك غیب گیری هم غیب دان بیابی

گنجی که تو شنیدی سودای آن گزیدی
گر در زمین ندیدی در آسمان بیابی

در عشق اگر امینی ای بس بتان چینی
هم رایگان ببینی هم رایگان بیابی

در آینه مبارك آن صاف صاف بی‌شك
نقش بهشت یك یك هم در جهان بیابی

چون تیر عشق خستت معشوق کرد مستت
گر جان بشد ز دستت صد همچنان بیابی

قفل طلسم مشکل سهلت شود به حاصل
گر از وساوس دل یك دم امان بیابی

درهم شکن بتان را از بهر شاه جان را
تا نقش بند آن را اندر عیان بیابی

تبریز در محقق از شمس ملت و حق
در رمزهای مطلق صد ترجمان بیابی

{ 7 }

peesh az aan kandar jahaan baaqh-e mey-o angoor bood,
az sharaab-e laayazaali jaan-e maa makhmoor bood

maa beh baqhdaad-e jahaan-e jaan an-al-haqh meezadeem
peesh az aan kin daar-o geer-o nokteh-ye mansoor bood

peesh az aan kin nafs-e kol dar aab-o gel me'maar shod,
dar kharaabaat-e haqhaayeqh eish-e maa ma'moor bood

jaan-e maa hamchon jahaan bod, jaam-e jaan chon aaftaab
az sharaab-e jaan jahaan taa gardan andar noor bood

saaqhiyaa, in mo'jebaan-e aab-o gel raa mast kon
taa bedaanad har yeki koo az cheh dowlat door bood

jaan fadaa-ye saaqhiyi kaz raaH-e jaan dar miresad
taa barandaazad meqhaab az har cheh aan mastoooor bood

maa dahaan-haa baaz maandeh peesh-e aan saaqhi kaz oo
khomr-haaye bee-khomaar o shaHd-e bee zanbood bood

yaa dahaan-e maa begeer ey saaqhi var ney faash shod
aancheh dar haftom zamin chon ganj-haa ganjoor bood

shaHr-e tabreez ar khabar daari begoo aan aHd raa
aan zamaan keh shams-e-din bee shams-e-din mashHoor bood

پیش از آن کاندر جهان باغ و می و انگور بود
از شراب لایزالی جان ما مخمور بود

ما به بغداد جهان جان اناالحق میزدیم
پیش از آن کاین دار و گیر و نکته‌ی منصور بود

پیش از آن کاین نفس کل در آب و گل معمار شد
در خرابات حقایق عیش ما معمور بود

جان ما همچون جهان بد جام جان چون آفتاب
از شراب جان جهان تا گردن اندر نور بود

ساقیا این معجبان آب و گل را مست کن
تا بداند هر یکی کاو از چه دولت دور بود

جان فدای ساقیی کز راه جان در میرسد
تا براندازد نقاب از هر چه آن مستور بود

ما دهانها باز مانده پیش آن ساقی کز او
خمرهای بی خمار و شهد بی زنبور بود

یا دهان ما بگیر ای ساقی ور نی فاش شد
آنچ در هفتم زمین چون گنجها گنجور بود

شهر تبریز ار خبر داری بگو آن عهد را
آن زمان کی شمس دین بی شمس دین مشهور بود

{ 8 }

baaz aamadam baaz aamadam, az peesh-e aan yaar aamadam
dar man negar dar man negar, baHr-e to qham-khaar aamadam

shaad aamadam shaad aamadam, az jomleh aazaad aamadam
chandin hezaaraan saal shod, taa man beh goftaar aamadam

aanjaa ravam aanjaa ravam, baalaa bodam baalaa ravam
baazam rahaan baazam rahaan, kinjaa beh-zenhaar aamadam

man morqh-e laahooti bodam, deedee keh naasooti shodam
daamash nadeedam naagahaan dar vey gereftaar aamadam

man noor-e paakam ey pesar, na moshteh khaakam mokhtasar
aakhar sadaf man neestam, man dorr-e shaHvaar aamadam

maa raa beh chashm-e sar mabin, maa raa beh chashm-e ser bebin
aanjaa biyaa maa raa bebin, kaanjaa sabok-baar aamadam

az chaar maadar bartaram, vaz haft aabaa neez ham
man gowhar-e kaani bodam kinjaa bedeedaar aamadam

yaaram beh baazaar aaamadast, chaalaak-o hoshyaar aamadast
var nah beh baazaaram chekaar, vey raa talabkaar aamadam

ey shams-e tabreezi nazar dar koll-e aalam key koni
kandar biyaabaan-e fanaa jaan-o del afgaar aamadam

{ ۸ }

بازآمدم بازآمدم از پیش آن یار آمدم
در من نِگر در من نِگر بهر تو غمخوار آمدم

شاد آمدم شاد آمدم از جمله آزاد آمدم
چندین هزاران سال شد تا من به گفتار آمدم

آن جا روم آن جا روم بالا بدم بالا روم
بازم رَهان بازم رَهان کاین جا به زنهار آمدم

من مرغ لاهوتی بُدم دیدی که ناسوتی شدم
دامَش ندیدم ناگهان در وی گرفتار آمدم

من نور پاکم ای پسر نه مشت خاکم مختصر
آخر صدف من نیستم من درّ شَهوار آمدم

ما را به چشم سَر مَبین ما را به چشم سِر ببین
آن جا بیا ما را ببین کان جا سبکبار آمدم

از چار مادر برترم وز هفت آبا نیز هم
من گوهر کانی بُدَم کاین جا به دیدار آمدم

یارم به بازار آمدست چالاک و هشیار آمدست
ور نه به بازارم چه کار وی را طلبکار آمدم

ای شمس تبریزی نظر در کل عالم کی کنی
کاندر بیابان فنا جان و دل افگار آمدم

95

{ 9 }

beh-rooz-e marg cho taaboot-e man ravaan baashad
gomaan mabar keh maraa dard-e in jahaan baashad

baraaye man to mager-yo magoo dareeqh dareeqh
beh daam-e deev dar-ofti, dareeqh aan baashad!

jenaazeh-am cho bebini magoo faraaqh faraaqh
maraa vesaal o molaaqhaat aan zamaan baashad

maraa beh goor sepaaree mago veda'a, veda'a,
keh goor pardeh-ye jam'iiyat-e janaan baashad

foroo shodan cho bedeedee bar-aamadan benegar
qhoroob shams-o qhamar raa cheraa ziyaan baashad?

to raa qhoroob namaayad, vali shorooqh bovad
laHad cho habs namaayad khalaas-e jaan baashad

kodaam daaneh foroo raft dar zamin keh narost?
cheraa beh daaneh-ye ensaanat in gamaan baashad?

kodaam dalv foroo raft-o por boroon naamad?
ze chaaH, yoosof-e jaan raa cheraa faqhaan baashad?

dahaan cho basti az in sooy, aan taraf bogshaa
keh haay-haaye to dar javv-e laamakaan baashad

to raa chonin benamaayad keh man beh khaak shodam
beh zir-e paaye man in haft aasemaan baashad

به روز مرگ چو تابوت من روان باشد
گمان مبر که مرا درد این جهان باشد

برای من تو مَگِریْ و مگو دریغ دریغ
به دام دیو درُافتی دریغ آن باشد

جنازه‌ام چو ببینی مگو فراق فراق
مرا وصال و ملاقات آن زمان باشد

مرا به گور سپاری مگو وداع وداع
که گور پرده‌ی جمعیت جنان باشد

فروشدن چو بدیدی برآمدن بنگر
غروب شمس و قمر را چرا زیان باشد

تو را غروب نماید، ولی شروق بود
لَحَد چو حبس نماید خلاص جان باشد

کدام دانه فرورفت در زمین که نرست
چرا به دانه‌ی انسانت این گُمان باشد

کدام دَلْو فرورفت و پُر برون نامد
زِ چاهْ یوسف جان را چرا فَغان باشد

دهان چو بستی از این سوی آن طرف بگشا
که های هویِ تو در جو لامکان باشد

تو را چنین بنماید که من به خاك شدم
به زیرِ پایِ من این هفت آسمان باشد

{ 10 }

soofiyi dar baaqh as baHr-e goshaad
soofiyaanieh rooy bar zaano nahaad

pas foroo raft oo beh khod andar noqhool
shod malool az soorat-e khaabash fozool

keh cheh khosbi, aakhar andar raz negar
in derakhtaan been-o aasaar-o khozar

amr-e haqh beshnow keh goftash anzaroo
sooye in aasaar-e raHmat aar roo

goft aasaarash delast ey bolhavass
aan boroon aasaar-e aasaar-ast o bass!

baaqh-haa vo sabzeh-haa dar eyn-e jaan
bar boroon aksash cho dar aab-e ravaan

aan khiyaal-e baaqh baashad andar aab
keh konad az lotf-e aab aan ezteraab

baaqh-haa vo miveh-haa andar delast
aks-e lotf-e aan barin aab-o gelast

gar naboodi aks-e aan sarv-e soroor
pas nakhaandi eezadash daar-ol-qhoroor

jomleh maqhrooraan barin aks aamadeh
bar gomaani kin bovad jannat-kadeh

meegoreezand az osool-e baaqh-haa
bar khiyaali mikonand aan laaqh-haa

chonkeh khaab-e qheflat aayadshaan besar
raast beenand-o che soodast aan nazar

ey khonok aan raa keh peesh az marg mord
ya'ni oo az asl-e in raz booy bord

{ ۱۰ }

صوفیی در باغ از بهر گشاد
صوفیانه روی بر زانو نهاد

پس فرو رفت او به خود اندر نغول
شد ملول از صورت خوابش فضول

که چه خسپی آخر اندر رز نگر
این درختان بین و آثار و خضر

امر حق بشنو که گفتست انظروا
سوی این آثار رحمت آر رو

گفت آثارش دلست ای بوالهوس
آن برون آثار آثارست و بس

باغها و سبزه‌ها در عین جان
بر برون عکسش چو در آب روان

آن خیال باغ باشد اندر آب
که کند از لطف آب آن اضطراب

باغها و میوه‌ها اندر دلست
عکس لطف آن برین آب و گلست

گر نبودی عکس آن سرو سرور
پس نخواندی ایزدش دار الغرور

جمله مغروران برین عکس آمده
بر گمانی کاین بود جنت‌کده

می‌گریزند از اصول باغها
بر خیالی می‌کنند آن لاغها

چونک خواب غفلت آیدشان به سر
راست بینند و چه سودست آن نظر

ای خنک آن را که پیش از مرگ مرد
یعنی او از اصل این رز بوی برد

99

{ 11 }

beh saaqhi dar negar, dar mast mangar
beh yoosof dar negar dar dast mangar

ayaa maahi-ye jaan dar shasht-e qhaaleb
bebin sayyaad raa, dar shast mangar

bedaan asli negar kaaqhaaz boodi
beh far'ii kaan konoon peyvast mangar

bedaan golzaar-e bee-paayaan nazar kon
bedin khaari keh paayat khast mangar

homaayi bin keh saayeh bar to afkand
beh zaaqhi kaz kaf-e to jast mangar

cho sarv-o sonboleh baalaa ravesh kon
banafsheh vaar sooye past mangar

cho dar jooyat ravaan shod aab-e heyvaan
beh khomm-o koozeh gar eshkast mangar

beh hasteebakhsh-o mastee-bakhsh begrow
manaal az neest, vandar hast mangar

qhanaa'at bin keh narrast-o sabok-row
beh tam'e maadeh-ye aabast mangar

to saafaan bin keh bar baalaa daveedand
beh dordi kaan beh-bon benshast mangar

jahaan por bin zeh soorat-haaye qhodsi
bedaan soorat keh raahat bast mangar

beh daam-e eshqh morqhaan-e shegerfand
beh boomi keh ze-daamash rast mangar

beH az to naateqhi andar kamin hast
dar aan kin laHzeh khaamooshast mangar

به ساقی درنگر در مست منگر
به یوسف درنگر در دست منگر

ایا ماهی جان در شست قالب
ببین صیاد را در شست منگر

بدان اصلی نگر کآغاز بودی
به فرعی کآن کنون پیوست منگر

بدان گلزار بی پایان نظر کن
بدین خاری که پایت خست منگر

همایی بین که سایه بر تو افکند
به زاغی کز کف تو جست منگر

چو سرو و سنبله بالاروش کن
بنفشه وار سوی پست منگر

چو در جویت روان شد آب حیوان
به خم و کوزه گر اشکست منگر

به هستی بخش و مستی بخش بگرو
منال از نیست و اندر هست منگر

قناعت بین که نرست و سبک رو
به طمع مادهٔ آبست منگر

تو صافان بین که بر بالا دویدند
به دردی کآن به بن بنشست منگر

جهان پر بین ز صورتهای قدسی
بدان صورت که راهت بست منگر

به دام عشق مرغان شگرفند
به بومی که ز دامش رست منگر

به از تو ناطقی اندر کمین هست
در آن کاین لحظه خاموشست منگر

{ 12 }

dar del khiyaalash zaan bovad taa to beh har soo nangari
vaan lotf-e bee-had zaan konad taa heech az had nagzari

baa soofiyaan-e saaf-din dar vajd gardee hamneshin
gar paay dar beeroon nehi zin khaaneqhaah-e shesh-dadri

daaree daree penhaan sefat, shesh dar majoo vo shesh jehat
penhaan dariee keh har shabee zaan dar hamee beeroon pari

chon meeparee bar paaye to reshtey khiyaalee basteh-and
taa vaakeshandat sobH-dam, taa bar naparree yeksari

baaz aa beh zendaan-e rahem taa khelqhatat kaamel shodan
hast in jahaan hamchon rahem, in jomleh khoon zaan meekhori

jaan raa cho bar rooyeed par, shod beyzeh-ye tan raa shekast
jaan ja'far-e tayyaar shod, taa meenamaayad ja'fari

در دل خیالش زآن بود تا تو به هر سو ننگری
وآن لطف بی‌حد زآن کند تا هیچ از حد نگذری

با صوفیان صاف دین در وجد گردی همنشین
گر پای در بیرون نهی زین خانقاه شش دری

داری دری پنهان صفت شش در مجو و شش جهت
پنهان دری که هر شبی زآن در همی‌بیرون پری

چون می‌پری بر پای تو رشته خیالی بسته‌اند
تا واکشندت صبحدم تا برنپری یك سری

بازآ به زندان رحم تا خلقتت کامل شدن
هست این جهان همچون رحم این جمله خون زآن می‌خوری

جان را چو بررویید پر شد بیضه‌ی تن را شکست
جان جعفر طیار شد تا می‌نماید جعفری

{ 13 }

in baar man yek-baaregee dar aasheqhee peecheedeh-am
in baar man yek-baaregee az aaafiyat bobreedeh-am

del raa ze khod bar-kandeh-am, baa cheez-e deegar zendeh-am
aqhl-o del-o andeesheh raa az beekh-o bon soozeedeh-am

ey mardomaan, ey mardomaan, az man nayaayad mardomee
deevaaneh ham naneedshad aan kandar del andeesheedeh-am

deevaaneh kowkab reekhteh az shoor-e man bogreekhteh
man baa ajal aameekhteh dar neestee parreedeh-am

emrooz aqhl-e man ze man yek-baaregee beezaar shod
khaahad keh tarsaanad maraa, pendaasht man naa-deedeh-am

man khod kojaa tarsam azoo? sheklee bekardam baHr-e oo
man geej kay baasham vali qhaased chonin geejeedeh-am

man az baraaye maslahat dar habs-e donyaa maandeh-am
habs az kojaa man az kojaa, maal-e keraa dozdeedeh-am?

dar habs-e tan qharqham beh khoon, vaz ashk-e chashm-e har haroon
daamaan-e khoonaalood raa dar khaak meemaaleedeh-am

maanand-e teflee dar shekam man parvaresh daaram ze khoon
yek baar zaayad aadami, man baarhaa zaayeedeh-am

to mast-e mast-e sar-khoshee, man mast-e bee-sar sar-khosham
to aasheqh-e khandaan-labee, man bee-dahaan khandeedeh-am

man torfeh-morqham kaz chaman, baa eshtehaaye kheeshtan
bee-daam-o bee geerandeh-ii andar qhafas kheezeedeh-am

zeeraa qhafas baa doostaan khosh-tar ze-baaqh-o boostan
baHr-e rezaaye yoosofaan dar chaaH aaraameedeh-am

این بار من یکبارگی در عاشقی پیچیده‌ام
این بار من یکبارگی از عافیت ببریده‌ام

دل را ز خود برکنده‌ام با چیز دیگر زنده‌ام
عقل و دل و اندیشه را از بیخ و بن سوزیده‌ام

ای مردمان ای مردمان از من نیاید مردمی
دیوانه هم نندیشد آن کاندر دل اندیشیده‌ام

دیوانه کوکب ریخته از شور من بگریخته
من با اجل آمیخته در نیستی پریده‌ام

امروز عقل من ز من یک بارگی بیزار شد
خواهد که ترساند مرا پنداشت من نادیده‌ام

من خود کجا ترسم از او شکلی بکردم بهر او
من گیج کی باشم ولی قاصد چنین گیجیده‌ام

من از برای مصلحت در حبس دنیا مانده‌ام
حبس از کجا من از کجا مال که را دزدیده‌ام

در حبس تن غرقم به خون وز اشک چشم هر حرون
دامان خون آلود را در خاک می مالیده‌ام

مانند طفلی در شکم من پرورش دارم ز خون
یک بار زاید آدمی من بارها زاییده‌ام

تو مست مست سرخوشی من مست بی‌سر سرخوشم
تو عاشق خندان لبی من بی‌دهان خندیده‌ام

من طرفه مرغم کز چمن با اشتهای خویشتن
بی‌دام و بی‌گیرنده‌ای اندر قفص خیزیده‌ام

زیرا قفس با دوستان خوشتر ز باغ و بوستان
بهر رضای یوسفان در چاه آرامیده‌ام

{ 14 }

baaz foroo reekht eshqh az daro divaar-e man
baaz beborreed band oshtor-e kindaar-e man

baar-e degar sheer-e eshqh panjeh-ye khoonin goshaad
teshneh-ye khoon gasht baaz in del-e sagsaar-e man

baaz sar-e maaH shod nobat-e divaanegist
aah keh soody nakard daanesh-e besyaar-e man

baar-e degar fetneh zaad jamreh-ye deegar fotaad
khaab-e maraa bast baaz delbar-e beedaar-e man

sabr-e maraa khaab bord, aqhl-e maraa aab bord
baar-e maraa yaar bord, taa cheh shavad kaar-e man

kheez degar-baar kheez, kheez keh shod rast-kheez
maayeh-ye sad rastkheez shoor-e degar-baar-e man

gar zeh khazaan golsetaan chon del-e aaseqh besookht
nak rokh-e aan golsetaan golshan-o golzaar-e man

baaqh-e jahaan sookhteh, baaqh-e del afrookhteh
sookhteh asraar-e baaqh, saakhteh asraar-e man

nobat-e eshrat reseed, ey tan-e maHboos-e man
khal'at-e sehhat resid, ey del-e beemaar-e man

peer-e kharaabaat hin, az jehat-e shokr-e in
row gero-ve mey beneH kherqheh vo dastaar-e man

{ ١٤ }

باز فروریخت عشق از در و دیوار من
باز ببرید بند اشتر کین دار من

بار دگر شیر عشق پنجه‌ی خونین گشاد
تشنه‌ی خون گشت باز این دل سگسار من

باز سر ماه شد نوبت دیوانگی است
آه که سودی نکرد دانش بسیار من

بار دگر فتنه زاد جمره‌ی دیگر فتاد
خواب مرا بست باز دلبر بیدار من

صبر مرا خواب برد عقل مرا آب برد
بار مرا یار برد تا چه شود کار من

خیز دگربار خیز خیز که شد رستخیز
مایه‌ی صد رستخیز شور دگربار من

گر ز خزان گلستان چون دل عاشق بسوخت
نک رخ آن گلستان گلشن و گلزار من

باغ جهان سوخته باغ دل افروخته
سوخته اسرار باغ ساخته اسرار من

نوبت عشرت رسید ای تن محبوس من
خلعت صحت رسید ای دل بیمار من

پیر خرابات هین از جهت شکر این
رو گرو می بنه خرقه و دستار من

{ 15 }

eshqh bin baa aasheqhaan aameekhteh
rooH bin baa khaakdaan aameekhteh

chand beenee een-o aan-o neek-o bad
bengar aakher een-o aan aameekhteh

chand gooyi bee-neshaan-o baa neshaan
bee-neshaan bin baa neshaan aameekhteh

chand gooyi in jahaan-o aan jahaan
aan jahaan bin vin jahaan aameekhteh

del cho shaah aamad zabaan chon tarjomaan
shaah bin baa tarjomaan aameekhteh

andar-aameezeed zeera baHr-e maast
in zamin baa aasemaan aameekhteh

aab-o aatash been-o khaak-o baad raa
doshmanaan chon doostan aameekhteh

gorg-o meesh-o sheer-o aaho chaar zed
az naheeb-e qhaHremaan aamikhteh

gar cheh kazhbaazand-o zeddaanand, leek
hamcho teerand-o kamaan aameekhteh

aan chonaan shaahi negar kaz lotf-e oo
khaar-o gol dal golsetaan aameekhteh

aan chonaan abri negar kaz feyz-e oo
aab-e chandin naavdaan aameekhteh

ettehaad andar asar been-o bedaan
nowbahaar-o meHregaan aameekhteh

qhand khaa khaamoosh baash-o heyf daan
qhand-o pand andar dahaan ameekhteh

Shams-e Tabrizi hami rooyad ze del
kas nabaashad aanchonaa aameekhteh

عشق بین با عاشقان آمیخته
روح بین با خاکدان آمیخته

چند بینی این و آن و نیك و بد
بنگر آخر این و آن آمیخته

چند گویی بی‌نشان و بانشان
بی‌نشان بین با نشان آمیخته

چند گویی این جهان و آن جهان
آن جهان بین وین جهان آمیخته

دل چو شاه آمد زبان چون ترجمان
شاه بین با ترجمان آمیخته

اندرآمیزید زیرا بهر ماست
این زمین با آسمان آمیخته

آب و آتش بین و خاك و باد را
دشمنان چون دوستان آمیخته

گرگ و میش و شیر و آهو چار ضد
از نهیب قهرمان آمیخته

گر چه کژبازند و ضدانند لیك
همچو تیرند و کمان آمیخته

آن چنان شاهی نگر کز لطف او
خار و گل در گلستان آمیخته

آن چنان ابری نگر کز فیض او
آب چندین ناودان آمیخته

اتحاد اندر اثر بین و بدان
نوبهار و مهرگان آمیخته

قند خا خاموش باش و حیف دان
قند و پند اندر دهان آمیخته

شمس تبریزی همی‌روید ز دل
کس نباشد آن چنان آمیخته

{ 16 }

in bol'ajab kandar khazaan shod aaftaab andar hamal
khoonam beh josh aamad konad dar joo-ye tan raqhs-oj-jamal

in raqhs-e mowj-e khoon negar, sahraa por az majnoon negar
vin eshrat-e bee-choon negar eeman ze shamsheer-e ajal

mordaar jaani mishavad, peeree javaani mishavad
mess zar-e kaani mishavad, dar shaHr-e maa na'm-al-badal

shaHri por az eshqh-o faraH, bar dast-e har masti qhadaH
in sooy noosh, aan sooy sah, in sooy sheer-o aan asal

dar shaHr yek soltaan bovad vin shaHr por soltaan ajab
bar charkh yek maahast-o bas, vin charkh por maah-o zohal

ro ro tabibaan raa begoo kaan jaa shomaa raa kaar neest
kaan jaa nabashad ellati, vaan jaa nabinad kas khelal

nee qhaazi-ii, ni shahneh-ii, ni meer-e shaHr-o moHtasab
bar aab-e daryaa kay ravad da'vee-yo khasmee-yo jadal?

این بوالعجب کاندر خزان شد آفتاب اندر حمل
خونم به جوش آمد کند در جوی تن رقص الجمل

این رقص موج خون نگر صحرا پر از مجنون نگر
وین عشرت بی‌چون نگر ایمن ز شمشیر اجل

مردار جانی می‌شود پیری جوانی می‌شود
مس زر کانی می‌شود در شهر ما نعم البدل

شهری پر از عشق و فرح بر دست هر مستی قدح
این سوی نوش آن سوی صح این جوی شیر و آن عسل

در شهر یک سلطان بود وین شهر پرسلطان عجب
بر چرخ یک ماهست بس وین چرخ پرماه و زحل

رو رو طبیبان را بگو کآنجا شما را کار نیست
کان جا نباشد علتی وان جا نبیند کس خلل

نی قاضیی نی شحنه‌ای نی میر شهر و محتسب
بر آب دریا کی رود دعوی و خصمی و جدل

{ 17 }

aqhl band-e raH-rovaanast ey pesar,
band beshkan, raH ayaanast ey pesar

aqhl band-o del fareeb-o jaan hejaab
raaH az in har seh nahaanast ey pesar

chon ze aqhl-o jaan-o del barkhaasti
in yaqhin ham dar gomaanast ey pesar

mard koo az khod naraft oo mard neest
eshqh-e bee dard aafsaanast ey pesar

seeneh-ye khod raa hadaf kon peesh-e doost
hin keh teerash dar kamaanast ey pesar

seeneh-ii kaz zakhm-e teerash khasteh shod
dar jabeenash sad neshaanast ey pesar

eshqh kaar-e naazokaan-e narm neest
eshqh kaar-e pahlevaanast ey pesar

har keh oo mar aasheqhaan raa bandeh shod
khosro-vo saaheb-qharaanast ey pesar

eshqh raa az kas mapors as eshqh pors
eshqh abr-e dor-feshaanast ey pesar

tarjomaani-ye manash mohtaaj neest
eshqh khod raa tarjomaanast ey pesar

gar ravi bar aasemaan-e haftomin
eshqh neekoo nardebaanast ey pesar

kar kojaa keh kaarevaani miravad
eshqh qhebley kaarevaanast ey pesar

in jahaan as eshqh taa nafribadat
kin jahaan az to jahaanast ey pesar

عقل بند ره روانست ای پسر
بند بشکن ره عیانست ای پسر

عقل بند و دل فریب و جان حجاب
راه از این هر سه نهانست ای پسر

چون ز عقل و جان و دل برخاستی
این یقین هم در گمانست ای پسر

مرد کاو از خود نرفت او مرد نیست
عشق بی درد آفسانست ای پسر

سینه‌ی خود را هدف کن پیش دوست
هین که تیرش در کمانست ای پسر

سینه‌ای کز زخم تیرش خسته شد
در جبینش صد نشانست ای پسر

عشق کار نازکان نرم نیست
عشق کار پهلوانست ای پسر

هر کی او مر عاشقان را بنده شد
خسرو و صاحب قرانست ای پسر

عشق را از کس مپرس از عشق پرس
عشق ابر درفشانست ای پسر

ترجمانی منش محتاج نیست
عشق خود را ترجمانست ای پسر

گر روی بر آسمان هفتمین
عشق نیکونردبانست ای پسر

هر کجا که کاروانی میرود
عشق قبله کاروانست ای پسر

این جهان از عشق تا نفریبدت
کاین جهان از تو جهانست ای پسر

{ 17 cont. }

hin dahaan barband-o khaamosh chon sadaf
kin zabaanat khasm-e jaanast ey pesar

Shams-e Tabriz aamad-o jaan shaademaan
chonkeh baa shamsash qheraanast ey pesar

﴿ ادامه ۱۷ ﴾

هین دهان بربند و خامش چون صدف
کاین زبانت خصم جانست ای پسر

شمس تبریز آمد و جان شادمان
چونک با شمسش قرانست ای پسر

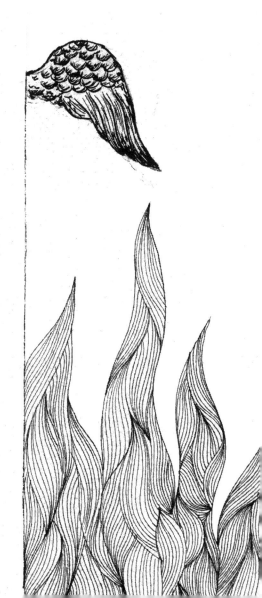

{ 18 }

benmaay rokh keh baaqh-o golestaanam aarezoost
bogshaay lab keh qhand-e faraavaanam aarezoost

ey aaftaab-e hosn, boroon aa damee ze abr
kaan cheHreh-ye mosha'sha'-e taabaanam aarezoost

beshnidam az havaaye to aavaaz-e tabl baaz
baaz aamadam keh saa'ad-e soltaanam aarezoost

gofti ze naaz, beesh maranjaan maraa, boro
aan goftanat keh beesh maranjaanam aarezoost

in naan-o aab-e charkh cho seylast bee-vafaa
man maahiyam, nahangam, ommaanam aarezoost

vallaH keh shaHr bee to maraa habs meeshavad
aavaaregi-yo kooH-o biyaabaanam aarezoost

zin hamrahaan-e sost-anaasor delam gereft
sheer-e khodaa vo na'areh-ye mastaanam aarezoost

jaanam malool gasht ze Fer'own-o zolm-e oo
aan noor-e rooye Moosiye Amraanam aarezoost

zin khalqh-e por shekaayat-e geryaan shodam malool
aan haay-hooy-o na'reh-ye mastaanam aareezost

yek dast jaam-e baadeh-vo yek dast ja'ad-e yaar
raqhsi chonin miyaaneh-ye meydaanam aarezoost

gooyaantaram ze bolbol, amaa ze rashk-e aam
moHrast bar dahaanam-o afqhaanam aarezoost

dee sheikh baa cheraaqh hamee gasht gerd-e shaHr
kaz deev-o dad maloolam-o ensaanam aarezoost

goftand yaaft mee-nashavad, josteh-eem maa
goft aan keh yaaft meenashavad, aanam aarezoost

بنمای رخ که باغ و گلستانم آرزوست
بگشای لب که قند فراوانم آرزوست

ای آفتاب حسن برون آ دمی ز ابر
کآن چهره‌ی مشعشع تابانم آرزوست

بشنیدم از هوای تو آواز طبل باز
باز آمدم که ساعد سلطانم آرزوست

گفتی ز ناز بیش مرنجان مرا برو
آن گفتنت که بیش مرنجانم آرزوست

این نان و آب و چرخ چو سیل‌ست بی‌وفا
من ماهیم نهنگم عمانم آرزوست

واللّه که شهر بی‌تو مرا حبس می‌شود
آوارگی و کوه و بیابانم آرزوست

زین همرهان سست عناصر دلم گرفت
شیر خدا و رستم دستانم آرزوست

جانم ملول گشت ز فرعون و ظلم او
آن نور روی موسی عمرانم آرزوست

زین خلق پرشکایت گریان شدم ملول
آن های هوی و نعره‌ی مستانم آرزوست

یک دست جام باده و یک دست جعد یار
رقصی چنین میانه‌ی میدانم آرزوست

گویاترم ز بلبل اما ز رشک عام
مهرست بر دهانم و افغانم آرزوست

دی شیخ با چراغ همی‌گشت گرد شهر
کز دیو و دد ملولم و انسانم آرزوست

گفتند یافت می‌نشود جسته‌ایم ما
گفت آن که یافت می‌نشود آنم آرزوست

{ 19 }

beekhod shodeh-am leekan beekhod-tar az in khaaham
baa chashm-e to migooyam man mast chonin khaaham

man taaj nemeekhaaham, man takht nemeekhaaham
dar khedmatat oftaadeh bar rooye zamin khaaham

aan yaar-e nekooye man begreft galooye man
goftaa keh che meekhaahi, goftam keh hamin khaaham

baa baad-e sabaa khaaham taa dam bezanam, leekan
chon man dam-e khod daaram, hamraaz-e mehin khaaham

dar halqheh-ye meeqhaatam, eeman shodeh z'aafaatam
moomam ze pey-e khatmat, z'aan naqhsh-e negin khaaham

maahee degar-ast ey jaan, andar del-e maH penhaan
zin elm yaqheenastam, aan eyn-e yaqhin khaaham

بیخود شده‌ام لیکن بیخودتر از این خواهم
با چشم تو می گویم من مست چنین خواهم

من تاج نمی‌خواهم من تخت نمی‌خواهم
در خدمتت افتاده بر روی زمین خواهم

آن یار نکوی من بگرفت گلوی من
گفتا که چه می خواهی گفتم که همین خواهم

با باد صبا خواهم تا دم بزنم لیکن
چون من ز دم خود دارم همراز مهین خواهم

در حلقه ی میقاتم ایمن شده ز آفاتم
مومم ز پی ختمت زان نقش نگین خواهم

ماهی دگر است ای جان اندر دل مه پنهان
زین علم یقینستم آن عین یقین خواهم

{ 20 }

kaar-e man een ast keh kaareem neest
aasheqham az eshqh-e to aareem neest

taa keh maraa sheer-e qhamat seyd kard
joz keh hamin sheer shekaareem neest

dar tak-e in baHr, cheh khosh gowhari
keh masal-e mowj, qharaareem neest

bar lab-e baHr-e to moqheemam, moqheem
mast-e labam gar cheh kenaareem neest

vaqhf konam eshkam-e khod bar meyat
kaz mey-e to heech khomaareem neest

meeresadam baadeh-ye to z'aasemaan
mennat-e har sheereh-feshaareem neest

baadeh-at az kooH sokoonat barad
eyb makon zaan keh vaqhaareem neest

molk-e jahaan geeram, chon aaftaab
gar cheh sepaahi-yo savaareem neest

gar cheh nadaaram beh jahaan sarvari
dard-e sar-e beehodeh baareem neest

bar sar-e kooye to maraa khaaneh geer
kaz sar-e kooye to gozaareem neest

hamcho shekar baa golat aameekhtam
neest ajab gar sar-e khaareem neest

qhotb-e jahaani, hameh raa roo beh tost
joz keh beh gerd-e to davaareem neest

کار من اینست که کاریم نیست
عاشقم از عشق تو عاریم نیست

تا که مرا شیر غمت صید کرد
جز که همین شیر شکاریم نیست

در تک این بحر چه خوش گوهری
که مثل موج قراریم نیست

بر لب بحر تو مقیمم مقیم
مست لبم گر چه کناریم نیست

وقف کنم اشکم خود بر میت
کز می تو هیچ خماریم نیست

می‌رسدم باده‌ی تو ز آسمان
منت هر شیره فشاریم نیست

باده‌ات از کوه سکونت برد
عیب مکن زان که وقاریم نیست

ملک جهان گیرم چون آفتاب
گر چه سپاهی و سواریم نیست

گر چه ندارم به جهان سروری
دردسر بیهده باریم نیست

بر سر کوی تو مرا خانه گیر
کز سر کوی تو گذاریم نیست

همچو شکر با گلت آمیختم
نیست عجب گر سر خاریم نیست

قطب جهانی همه را رو به توست
جز که به گرد تو دواریم نیست

{ 20 cont. }

kheesh-e man aanast keh az eshqh zaad
khoshtar az in kheesh-o tabaareem neest

chist fozoon az do jahaan? shaHr-e eshqh!
beHtar az in shaHr-o diyaareem neest

gar nanegaaram sokhanee ba'ad azin,
neest az aan roo keh negaareem neest

خویش من آنست که از عشق زاد
خوشتر از این خویش و تباریم نیست

چیست فزون از دو جهان شهر عشق
بهتر از این شهر و دیاریم نیست

گر ننگارم سخنی بعد از این
نیست از آن رو که نگاریم نیست

{ 21 }

haleh nowmeed nabaashee keh toraa yaar beraanad
garat emrooz beraanad, nah keh fardaat bekhaanad?

dar agar bar to bebandad, maro vo sabr kon aanjaa
ze pas-e sabr to raa oo beh sar-e sadr neshaanad

va agar bar to bebandad hameh raH haa vo gozar haa
raH-e penhaan benamaayad keh kas aan raaH nadaanad

hah keh qhassaaab beh khanjar cho sar-e meesh beborrad
nahelad koshteh-ye khod raa koshad aan gaah keshaanad

cho dam-e mish namaanad ze dam-e khod konadash por
to bebeenee dam-e yazdaan beh kojaahaat resaanad

beh masal goftam in raa vo agar nah karam-e oo
nakoshad heech kasee raa vo zeh koshtan berahaanad

hamegee molk-e Soleymaan beh yekee moor bebakhshad
bedehad har do jahaan raa vo delee raa naramaanad

del-e man gerd-e jahaan gasht-o nayaabeed mesaalash
beh keh maanad beh keh maanad beh keh maanad beh keh maanad

haleh khamoosh, keh bee goft, az in mey hamegaan raa
becheshaanad, becheshaanad, becheshaanad, becheshaanad

هله نومید نباشی که تو را یار براند
گرت امروز براند نه که فردات بخواند

در اگر بر تو ببندد مرو و صبر کن آن جا
ز پس صبر تو را او به سر صدر نشاند

و اگر بر تو ببندد همه رهها و گذرها
ره پنهان بنماید که کس آن راه نداند

نه که قصاب به خنجر چو سر میش ببرد
نهلد کشته خود را کشد آن گاه کشاند

چو دم میش نماند ز دم خود کندش پر
تو بینی دم یزدان به کجاهات رساند

به مثل گفتم این را و اگر نه کرم او
نکشد هیچ کسی را و ز کشتن برهاند

همگی ملک سلیمان به یکی مور ببخشد
بدهد هر دو جهان را و دلی را نرماند

دل من گرد جهان گشت و نیابید مثالش
به کی ماند به کی ماند به کی ماند به کی ماند

هله خاموش که بی گفت از این می همگان را
بچشاند بچشاند بچشاند

{ 22 }

talkhee nakonad sheerin zaqhanam
khaalee nakonad az mey dahanam

oryaan konadam har sobH-dami
gooyad keh biyaa, man jaameh kanam

dar khaaneh jahad, mohlat nadehad
oo bas nakonad, pas man cheh konam?

az saaqhar-e oo geej-ast saram
az deedan-e oo jaan ast tanam

tang ast bar-oo har haft falaak
chon meeravad oo dar peerhanam?

az sheereh-ye oo man sheer-delam
dar arbadeh-ash sheerin sokhanam

meegoft keh to dar chang-e mani
man saakhtamant, choonat nazanam?

man chang-e to-am, bar har rag-e man
to zakhmeh zani, man tan tananam

haasel to ze man del bar nakani
del neest maraa, man khod cheh konam?

تلخی نکند شیرین ذقنم
خالی نکند از می دهنم

عریان کندم هر صبحدمی
گوید که بیا من جامه کنم

در خانه جهد مهلت ندهد
او بس نکند پس من چه کنم

از ساغر او گیج است سرم
از دیدن او جان است تنم

تنگ است بر او هر هفت فلک
چون می رود او در پیرهنم

از شیره ی او من شیردلم
در عربده اش شیرین سخنم

می گفت که تو در چنگ منی
من ساختمت چونت نزنم

من چنگ توام بر هر رگ من
تو زخمه زنی من تن تننم

حاصل تو ز من دل برنکنی
دل نیست مرا من خود چه کنم

{ 23 }

andak-andak jam-'e mastaan meeresand
andak-andak mey-parastaan meeresand

del-navaazaan naaz-naazaan dar rahand
gol-ezaaraan az golestaan meeresand

andak andak zin jahaan-e hast-o neest
neestaan raftand-o hastaan meeresand

jomleh daaman-haaye por zar hamcho kaan
az baraaye tangdastaan meeresand

laaqharaan-e khasteh az mar'aa-ye eshqh
farbehaan-o tandorostaan meeresand

jaan-e paakaan chon sho'aa'e aaftaab
az chonaan baalaa beh pastaan meeresand

khorram aan baaqhi keh baHr-e maryamaan
meeveh-haaye no-zemestaan meeresand

asleshaan lotfast-o ham vaa-gasht-e lotf
ham ze bostaan sooye bostaan meeresand

اندك اندك جمع مستان می‌رسند
اندك اندك می پرستان می‌رسند

دلنوازان نازنازان در ره اند
گلعذاران از گلستان می‌رسند

اندك اندك زین جهان هست و نیست
نیستان رفتند و هستان می‌رسند

جمله دامن‌های پرزر همچو کان
از برای تنگدستان می‌رسند

لاغران خسته از مرعای عشق
فربهان و تندرستان می‌رسند

جان پاکان چون شعاع آفتاب
از چنان بالا به پستان می‌رسند

خرم آن باغی که بهر مریمان
میوه‌های نو زمستان می‌رسند

اصلشان لطفست و هم واگشت لطف
هم ز بستان سوی بستان می‌رسند

{ 24 }

har damee fekree cho meHmaan-e azeez
aayad andar seeneh-at har rooz neez

fekr-e qham gar raaH-e shaadee meezanad
kaar-saazi-haa-ye shaadee meekonad

khaaneh meeroobad beh tondee too ze-qheyr
taa dar aayad shaadi-ye no z'asl-e kheyr

meefeshaanad barg-e zard az shaakh-e del
taa berooyad barg-e sabz-e mottasel

mikanad beekh-e soroor-e koHneh raa
taa kharaamad zowqh-e no az maavaraa

qham kanad beekh-e kazh-e pooseedeh raa
taa namaayad beekh-e roo poosheedeh raa

qham ze del har cheh bereezad yaa barad
dar avaz haqhqhaa keh beHtar aavarad

khaaseh aan raa keh yagheenash baashad in
keh bovad qham bandeh-ye aHl-e yagheen

gar torosh-rooyi nayaarad abr-o barqh
raz besoozad az tabassom-haaye sharqh

fekr dar seeneh dar-aayad no-beh-no
khand-khandaan beesh-e oo to baaz row

هر دمی فکری چو مهمان عزیز
آید اندر سینه‌ات هر روز نیز

فکر غم گر راه شادی می‌زند
کارسازیهای شادی می‌کند

خانه می‌روبد به تندی او ز غیر
تا در آید شادی نو ز اصل خیر

می‌فشاند برگ زرد از شاخ دل
تا بروید برگ سبز متصل

می‌کند بیخ سرور کهنه را
تا خرامد ذوق نو از ماورا

غم کند بیخ کژ پوسیده را
تا نماید بیخ رو پوشیده را

غم ز دل هر چه بریزد یا برد
در عوض حقا که بهتر آورد

خاصه آن را که یقینش باشد این
که بود غم بنده‌ی اهل یقین

گر ترش‌رویی نیارد ابر و برق
رز بسوزد از تبسمهای شرق

فکر در سینه در آید نو به نو
خند خندان پیش او تو باز رو

{ 25 }

tadbeer konad bandeh vo taghdeer nadaanad
tadbeer beh taghdeer-e khodaavand cheh maanad?

bandeh cho biyandeeshad, peydaast cheh beenad
heelat bekonad leek khodaayi benadaanad

gaami do chonaan aayad koo rast nahaadast
vaan gaaH keh daanad keh kojaahaash keshaanad

esteezeh makon, mamlekat-e eshqh talab kon
kin mamlekatat az malak-ol-mowt rahaanad

shaH raa to shekaari show, kam geer shekaari
k'eshkaar-e to raa baaz-e ajal baaz setaanad

khaamosh kon-o bogzin to yeki jaaye qharaari
k'aan jaa keh gozeenee malak aan jaat neshsaanad

تدبیر کند بنده و تقدیر نداند
تدبیر به تقدیر خداوند چه ماند

بنده چو بیندیشد پیداست چه بیند
حیلت بکند لیک خدایی بنداند

گامی دو چنان آید کاو راست نهادست
وان گاه که داند که کجاهاش کشاند

استیزه مکن مملکت عشق طلب کن
کاین مملکتت از ملک الموت رهاند

شه را تو شکاری شو کم گیر شکاری
کاشکار تو را باز اجل بازستاند

خامش کن و بگزین تو یکی جای قراری
کان جا که گزینی ملک آن جات نشاند

{ 26 }

bar neveshteh heech benveesad kasee?
yaa nahaaleh kaarad andar maqhrasee ?

kaaqhazee jooyad keh aan benveshteh neest
tokhm kaarad mowze-'ee keh keshteh neest

to baraadar mowze-'eh naakeshteh baash
kaaqhaz-e espeed-e naa-benveshteh baash

taa mosharraf gardi az noon-ol-qhalam
ta bekaarad dar to tokhm aan zol-karam

{ ٢٦ }

بر نوشته هیچ بنویسد کسی
یا نهاله کارد اندر مغرسی

کاغذی جوید که آن بنوشته نیست
تخم کارد موضعی که کشته نیست

تو برادر موضع ناکشته باش
کاغذ اسپید نابنوشته باش

تا مشرف گردی از نون والقلم
تا بکارد در تو تخم آن ذوالکرم

{ 27 }

bejoosheed, bejoosheed, keh maa aHl-e sho'aareem
bejoz eshqh, bejoz eshqh, degar kaar nadaareem

dar in khaak, dar in khaak, dar in mazra'eh-ye paak,
bejoz meHr, bejoz eshqh, degar tokhm nakaareem

cheh masteem, cheh masteem, az aan shaaH keh hasteem,
biyaayeed, biyaayeed, keh taa dast bar-aareem

cheh daaneem, cheh daaneem, keh maa doosh cheh khordeem
keh emrooz hameh rooz, khameereem-o khomaareem

maporseed, maproseed, ze aHvaal-e haqhiqhat
keh maa baadeh parasteem, nah peymaaneh shomaareem

shomaa mast nagashteed, vazaan baadeh nakhordeed
cheh daaneed, cheh daaneed, keh maa dar cheh shekaareem

nayofteem, bar in khaak setaan maa na haseereem
baraayeem, bar in charkh keh maa mard-e hesaareem!

بجوشید بجوشید که ما اهل شعاریم
بجز عشق بجز عشق دگر کار نداریم

در این خاک دراین خاک در این مزرعه‌ی پاک
بجز مهر بجز عشق دگر تخم نکاریم

چه مستیم چه مستیم از آن شاه که هستیم
بیایید بیایید که تا دست برآریم

چه دانیم چه دانیم که ما دوش چه خوردیم
که امروز همه روز خمیریم و خماریم

مپرسید مپرسید ز احوال حقیقت
که ما باده پرستیم نه پیمانه شماریم

شما مست نگشتید وزآن باده نخوردید
چه دانید چه دانید که ما در چه شکاریم

نیفتیم بر این خاک ستان ما نه حصیریم
برآییم بر این چرخ که ما مرد حصاریم

{ 28 }

chand nahaan daari aan khandeh raa?
aan maH-e taabandeh-ye farkhondeh raa?

bandeh konad roo-ye to sad shaaH raa
shaaH konad khandeh-ye to bandeh raa

khandeh biyaamooz gol-e sorkh raa
jelveh kon aan dowlat-e paayandeh raa

basteh bedaanast dar-e aasemaan
taa bekeshad chon to goshaayandeh raa

deedeh-ye qhattaar, shotor-haa-ye mast
montazeraanand keshaanandeh raa

zolf bar-afshaan-o dar aan halqheh kesh
halqh-e do-sad halqheh-robaayandeh raa

rooz-e vesaalast-o sanam haazerast
heech mapaa moddat-e aayandeh raa

aasheqh-e zakhmast, daf-e sakht-roo
meyl-e labast aan ney-e naalandeh raa

bar rokh-e daf chand tapaancheh bezan
dam deH aan naay-e segaalandeh raa

gar beh tama' naaleh bar-aarad robaab
khosh begoshaa aan kaf-e bakhshandeh raa

eyb makon gar qhazal abtar bemaand
neest vafaa khaater-e parrandeh raa

چند نهان داری آن خنده را
آن مه تابنده‌ی فرخنده را

بنده کند روی تو صد شاه را
شاه کند خنده‌ی تو بنده را

خنده بیاموز گل سرخ را
جلوه کن آن دولت پاینده را

بسته بدانست در آسمان
تا بکشد چون تو گشاینده را

دیده‌ی قطار شترهای مست
منتظرانند کشاننده را

زلف برافشان و در آن حلقه کش
حلق دو صد حلقه رباینده را

روز وصالست و صنم حاضرست
هیچ مپا مدت آینده را

عاشق زخمست دف سخت رو
میل لبست آن نی نالنده را

بر رخ دف چند طپانچه بزن
دم ده آن نای سگالنده را

ور به طمع ناله برآرد رباب
خوش بگشا آن کف بخشنده را

عیب مکن گر غزل ابتر بماند
نیست وفا خاطر پرنده را

{ 29 }

aatashi no dar vojood andar zadeem
dar miyaan-e maHv-e no andar shodeem

neek-o bad andar jahaan-e hastiyast
maa na neekeem ey baraadar na badeem

har che charkh-e dozd az maa bordeh bood
shab asass rafteem-o az vey bestadeem

maa yekee boodeem baa sad maa vo man
yek jovi zaan yek namaand-o maa sadim

az khodee naarafteh natvaan aamadan
az khodee rafteem, vaangah aamdadim

qhadd-e maa shod past andar qhadd-e eshqh
qhadd-e maa chon past shod, aali qhadeem

peeisheh-ye mardi zeh haqh aamookhtim
paHlevaan-e eshq-o yaar-e aHmadeem

bist-o noH harf-ast bar lowH-e vojood
harf-haa shosteem-o andar abjadeem

sa'ad-e Shamseddin-e Tabrizi betaaft
vaz qheraan-e sa'ad-e oo maa as'adeem

آتشی نو در وجود اندرزدیم
در میان محو نو اندرشدیم

نیك و بد اندر جهان هستی است
ما نه نیكیم ای برادر نی بدیم

هر چه چرخ دزد از ما برده بود
شب عسس رفتیم و از وی بستدیم

ما یكی بودیم با صد ما و من
یك جوی زان یك نماند و ما صدیم

از خودی نارفته نتوان آمدن
از خودی رفتیم وانگه آمدیم

قد ما شد پست اندر قد عشق
قد ما چون پست شد عالی قدیم

پیشه‌ی مردی ز حق آموختیم
پهلوان عشق و یار احمدیم

بیست و نه حرف است بر لوح وجود
حرف‌ها شستیم و اندر ابجدیم

سعد شمس الدین تبریزی بتافت
وز قران سعد او ما اسعدیم

{ 30 }

maraa aHdeest baa shaadi keh shaadi aan-e man baashad
maraa ghowleest baa jaanaan keh jaanaan jaan-e man baashad

beh dast-e kheeshtan farmaan beh dastam daad aan soltaan
keh taa takhtast o taa bakhtast, oo soltaan-e man baashad

agar hoshyaar agar mastam nageerad qheyr-e oo dastam
vagar man dast-e khod khastam ham-oo darmaan-e man baash

cheh zaHreh daarad anidsheh keh gerd-e shahr-e man gardad
keh qhasd-e molk-e man daarad cho oo kaaqhaan-e man baash

nabeenad roo-ye man zardee beh eqhbaal-e lab-e la'lash
bemeerad peesh-e man Rostam cho oo dastaan-e man baashad

bedarram zaHreh-ye zoHreh, kharaasham maah raa cheHreh
baram az aasemaan moHreh cho oo keyvaan-e man baashad

cheraaqh-e charkh-e gardoonam cho ojri-khaar-e khorsheedam
ameer-e gooy-o chowgaanam cho del meydaan-e man baashad

manam Mesr-o shekar-khaaneh cho Yoosof dar baram geeram
cheh jooyam molk-e Kan'aan raa cho oo Kan'aan-e man baasha

zaHi haazer, zaHi naazer, zaHi haafez, zaHi naaser
zaHi elzaam-e har monker, cho oo borhaan-e man baashad

yeki jaaneest dar aalam keh nangash aayad as soorat
bepooshad soorat-e ensaan valee ensaan-e man baashad

مرا عهدیست با شادی که شادی آن من باشد
مرا قولیست با جانان که جانان جان من باشد

به خط خویشتن فرمان به دستم داد آن سلطان
که تا تختست و تا بختست او سلطان من باشد

اگر هشیار اگر مستم نگیرد غیر او دستم
وگر من دست خود خستم هم او درمان من باشد

چه زهره دارد اندیشه که گرد شهر من گردد
که قصد ملک من دارد چو او خاقان من باشد

نبیند روی من زردی به اقبال لب لعلش
بمیرد پیش من رستم چو او دستان من باشد

بدرم زهره‌ی زهره خراشم ماه را چهره
برم از آسمان مهره چو او کیوان من باشد

چراغ چرخ گردونم چو اجری خوار خورشیدم
امیر گوی و چوگانم چو دل میدان من باشد

منم مصر و شکرخانه چو یوسف در برم گیرم
چه جویم ملک کنعان را چو او کنعان من باشد

زهی حاضر زهی ناظر زهی حافظ زهی ناصر
زهی الزام هر منکر چو او برهان من باشد

یکی جانیست در عالم که ننگش آید از صورت
بپوشد صورت انسان ولی انسان من باشد

eyshhaataan noosh baadaa har zamaan ey aasheqhaan
vaz shomaa kaan-e shekar baad in jahaan ey aasheqhaan

noosh-o joosh-e aasheqhaan taa arsh-o taa korsee reseed
bargozasht az arsh-o farsh in kaaravaan ey aasheqhaan

az lab-e daryaa cheh gooyam, lab nadaarad baHr-e jaan
bar-fozoodast az makaan-o laamakaan ey aasheqhaan

maa mesaal-e mowj-haa andar qhiyaam-o dar sojood
taa bedid aayad neshaan az bee-neshaan ey aasheqhaan

gar kasi porsad kiyaaneed ey sar-andaazaan shomaa
hin begooyeedash keh jaan-e jaan-e jaan, ey aasheqhaan

gar kasi qhavaas nabvad baHr-e jaan bakhshandeh ast
koo hami bakhshad gohar-haa raayegaan ey aasheqhaan

in chonin shod v'aan chonaan shod, khalqh raa dar hoqheh kard
baaz rasteem az choneen-o az chonaan ey aasheqhaan

zeer-e paaye man gol-ast-o zeer-e paahaashaan gel-ast
chon bekoobam paa miyaan-e monkeraan ey aasheqhaan

khorramaa aan dam keh az masti-ye jaanaan jaan-e maa
minadaanad aasemaan az reesmaan ey aasheqhaan

torfeh daryaayi mo'allaqh aamad in daryaaye eshqh
nee beh zeer-o nee beh balaa, nee miyaan ey aasheqhaan

taa bedeed aamad sho'aa'eh Shams-e Tabrizi ze sharqh
jaan-e motlaqh shod zameen-o aasemaan ey aasheqhaan

عیشهاتان نوش بادا هر زمان ای عاشقان
وز شما کان شکر باد این جهان ای عاشقان

نوش و جوش عاشقان تا عرش و تا کرسی رسید
برگذشت از عرش و فرش این کاروان ای عاشقان

از لب دریا چه گویم لب ندارد بحر جان
برفزودست از مکان و لامکان ای عاشقان

ما مثال موجها اندر قیام و در سجود
تا بدید آید نشان از بی نشان ای عاشقان

گر کسی پرسد کیانید ای سراندازان شما
هین بگوییدش که جان جان جان ای عاشقان

گر کسی غواص نبود بحر جان بخشنده است
کاو همی بخشد گهرها رایگان ای عاشقان

این چنین شد وان چنان شد خلق را در حقه کرد
بازرستیم از چنین و از چنان ای عاشقان

زیر پای من گل است و زیر پاهاشان گل است
چون بکوبم پا میان منکران ای عاشقان

خرما آن دم که از مستی جانان جان ما
می نداند آسمان از ریسمان ای عاشقان

طرفه دریایی معلق آمد این دریای عشق
نی به زیر و نی به بالا نی میان ای عاشقان

تا بدید آمد شعاع شمس تبریزی ز شرق
جان مطلق شد زمین و آسمان ای عاشقان

{ 32 }

man qholaam-e qhamaram qheyr-e qhamar heech magoo
peesh-e man joz sokhan-e sham'o shekar heech magoo

sokhan-e ranj magoo, joz sokhan-e ganj magoo
var azin bee-khabaree ranj mabar heech magoo

doosh deevaaneh shodam, eshqh maraa deed-o begoft:
aamadam, na'areh mazan, jaameh madar, heech magoo

goftam ey eshqh, man az cheez-e degar meetarsam
goft aan cheez-e degar neest, degar heech magoo

man beh goosh-e to sokhan-haaye nahaan khaaham goft
sar bejonbaan keh balee, joz keh beh sar heech magoo

qhamaree jaan-sefatee dar raH-e del peydaa shod
dar raH-e del cheh lateefast safar, heech magoo

goftam ey del cheh maHast in, del eshsaarat meekard
keh na andaazeh-ye tost in, begozar, heech magoo.

goftam in rooy-e fereshtast, ajab, yaa basharast?
goft in qheyr-e fereshtast-o bashar, heech magoo

goftam in cheest, begoo zeer-o zebar khaaham shod!
goft, meebaash chonin zeer-o zebar, heech magoo

ey neshasteh to dar in khaaneh-ye por naqhsh-o khiyaal
khiz az in khaaneh boro, rakht bebar, heech magoo.

goftam ey del pedaree kon, nah keh in vasf-e khodaast?
goft in hast, vali jaan-e pedar heech magoo

من غلام قمرم غیر قمر هیچ مگو
پیش من جز سخن شمع و شکر هیچ مگو

سخن رنج مگو جز سخن گنج مگو
ور از این بی‌خبری رنج مبر هیچ مگو

دوش دیوانه شدم عشق مرا دید و بگفت
آمدم نعره مزن جامه مدر هیچ مگو

گفتم ای عشق من از چیز دگر می‌ترسم
گفت آن چیز دگر نیست دگر هیچ مگو

من به گوش تو سخن‌های نهان خواهم گفت
سر بجنبان که بلی جز که به سر هیچ مگو

قمری جان صفتی در ره دل پیدا شد
در ره دل چه لطیف است سفر هیچ مگو

گفتم ای دل چه مه‌ست این دل اشارت می‌کرد
که نه اندازه‌ی توست این بگذر هیچ مگو

گفتم این روی فرشته‌ست عجب یا بشر است
گفت این غیر فرشته‌ست و بشر هیچ مگو

گفتم این چیست بگو زیر و زبر خواهم شد
گفت می‌باش چنین زیر و زبر هیچ مگو

ای نشسته تو در این خانه‌ی پرنقش و خیال
خیز از این خانه برو رخت ببر هیچ مگو

گفتم ای دل پدری کن نه که این وصف خداست
گفت این هست ولی جان پدر هیچ مگو

{ 33 }

har nafas aavaaz-e eshgh meeresad az chappo raast
maa beh falak meeraveem, azm-e tamaashaa keraast?

maa beh falak boodeh-eem, yaar-e malak boodeh-eem
baaz hamaanjaa raveem, jomleh keh aan shaHr-e maast

khod ze falak bartareem vaz malak afzoontareem
zin do cheraa nagzareem? manzel-e maa kebriyaast!

gowhar-e paak az kojaa, aalam-e khaak az kojaa?
bar cheh forood aamadeed? baar koneed in cheh jaast?

bakht-e javaan yaar-e maa, daadan-e jaan kaar-e maa
qhaafeleh-saalaar-e maa fakhr-e jahaan, mostaafaast!

booye khosh-e in naseem az shekan-e zolf-e oost
sha'sha'eh-ye in khiyaal, zaan rokh-e chon val-zahaast

dar del-e maa dar negar, har dam shaqh-e qhamar
kaz nazar-e aan nazar, chashm-e to aan soo cheraast?

khalqh cho morqhaabiyaan, zaadeh ze daryaa-ye jaan
kay konad in jaa maqhaam morqh kaz aan baHr khaast?

balkeh beh daryaa dareem, jomleh dar oo haazereem,
var nah ze daryaaye del, mowj peyaapey cheraast?

aamad mowj-e alast, keshtiye qhaaleb bebast
baaz cho keshti shekast, nowbat-e vasl-o laqhaast

هر نفس آواز عشق می‌رسد از چپ و راست
ما به فلک می‌رویم عزم تماشا کراست

ما به فلک بوده‌ایم یار ملک بوده‌ایم
باز همان جا رویم جمله که آن شهر ماست

خود ز فلک برتریم وز ملک افزونتریم
زین دو چرا نگذریم منزل ما کبریاست

گوهر پاک از کجا عالم خاک از کجا
بر چه فرود آمدیت بار کنید این چه جاست

بخت جوان یار ما دادن جان کار ما
قافله سالار ما فخر جهان مصطفاست

بوی خوش این نسیم از شکن زلف اوست
شعشعه‌ی این خیال زان رخ چون والضحاست

در دل ما درنگر هر دم شق قمر
کز نظر آن نظر چشم تو آن سو چراست

خلق چو مرغابیان زاده ز دریای جان
کی کند این جا مقام مرغ کز آن بحر خاست

بلک به دریا دریم جمله در او حاضریم
ور نه ز دریای دل موج پیاپی چراست

آمد موج الست کشتی قالب ببست
باز چو کشتی شکست نوبت وصل و لقاست

{ 34 }

nowbat-e vasl-o laqhaast, nowbat-e hashr-o baqhaast
nowbat-e lotf-o ataast, baHr-e safaa dar safaast

darj-e ataa shod padeed, qhorreh-ye daryaa reseed
sobH-e sa'aadat dameed, sobH cheh? noor-e khodaast!

soorat-o tasveer keest? in shaH-o in meer keest?
in kherad-e peer keest? in hameh roopoosh-haast!

chaareh-ye roopoosh-haa, hast chonin joosh-haa
cheshmeh-ye in noosh-haa dar sar-o chashm-e shomaast

dar sar-e khod peech, leek, hast shomaa raa dosar
in sar-e khaak az zamin, vaan sar-e paak az samaast

ey bas sar-haaye paak reekhteh dare paaye khaak
taa to bedaani keh sar zaan sar-e deegar beh-paast

aan sar-e aslee nahaan, vaan sar-e far'ee ayaan
daankeh pas-e in jahaan, aalam-e bee-montahaast

mashk beband ey saqhaa, mee-nabarad khonb-e maa
koozeh-ye edraak haa tang azin tangnaast

az sooye Tabriz taaft Shams-e haqh-o goftamash
noor-e to ham mottasel baa hameh vo ham jodaast

{ ٣٤ }

نوبت وصل و لقاست نوبت حشر و بقاست
نوبت لطف و عطاست بحر صفا در صفاست

درج عطا شد پدید غرهٔ دریا رسید
صبح سعادت دمید صبح چه نور خداست

صورت و تصویر کیست این شه و این میر کیست
این خرد پیر کیست این همه روپوش‌هاست

چارهٔ روپوش‌ها هست چنین جوش‌ها
چشمهٔ این نوش‌ها در سر و چشم شماست

در سر خود پیچ لیک هست شما را دو سر
این سر خاك از زمین وان سر پاك از سماست

ای بس سرهای پاك ریخته در پای خاك
تا تو بدانی که سر زان سر دیگر به پاست

آن سر اصلی نهان وآن سر فرعی عیان
دانك پس این جهان عالم بی‌منتهاست

مشك ببند ای سقا می‌نبرد خنب ما
کوزهٔ ادراك‌ها تنگ از این تنگناست

از سوی تبریز تافت شمس حق و گفتمش
نور تو هم متصل با همه و هم جداست

{ 35 }

har nafas aavaaz-e eshgh meeresad as chapp-o raast
maa beh chaman meeraveem, azm-e tamaashaa keraast?

nowbat-e khaaneh gozasht, nobat-e bostaan reseed
sobH-e sa'aadat dameed, vaght-e vesaal-o lahgaast

ey shaH-e saahebgheraan, kheez ze khaab-e geraan
markab-e dowlat beraan, nowbat-e vasl aan-e maast

tabl-e vafaa kooftand, raaH-e samaa rooftand
eysh-e shomaa naaghd shod, nesyeh-ye fardaa kojaast?

room bar-aavard dast, zangi-ye shab raa shekast
aalam-e baala vo past, por lama'aan-o safaast

ey khonok aan raa keh oo rast az in rang-o boo
zaankeh joz in rang-o boo dar del-o jaan rang-haast

ey khonok aan jaan-o del koo rahad az aab-o gel
gar cheh dar-in aab-o gel dastgaH-e keemiyaast

هر نفس آواز عشق می رسد از چپ و راست
ما به چمن می رویم عزم تماشا کراست

نوبت خانه گذشت نوبت بستان رسید
صبح سعادت دمید وقت وصال و لقاست

ای شه صاحب قران خیز ز خواب گران
مرکب دولت بران نوبت وصل آن ماست

طبل وفا کوفتند راه سما روفتند
عیش شما نقد شد نسیه‌ی فردا کجاست

روم برآورد دست زنگی شب را شکست
عالم بالا و پست پرلمعان و صفاست

ای خنک آن را که او رست از این رنگ و بو
زانک جز این رنگ و بو در دل و جان رنگ هاست

ای خنک آن جان و دل کو رهد از آب و گل
گر چه در این آب و گل دستگه کیمیاست

{ 36 }

aab zaneed raaH raa hin keh negaar meeresad
mozhdeh daheed baaqh raa booye bahaar meeresad

raaH daheed yaar raa aan maH-e daH-chahaar raa
kaz rokh-e noor-bakhsh-e oo noor nesaar meeresad

chaak shodast aasemaan qholqholeh-eest dar jahaan
anbar-o moshk meedamad sanjaqh-e yaar meeresad

rownaqh-e baaqh meeresad chashm-o cheraaqh meeresad
qham beh kenaareh meeravad maH beh kenaar meeresad

teer ravaaneh meeravad soo-ye neshaaneh meeravad
maa cheh neshasteh-eem pas shaH be-shekaar meeresad

baaqh salaam meekonad sarv qhiyaam meekonad
sabzeh piyaadeh meeravad qhoncheh savaar meeresad

khalvatiyaan-e aasemaan taa cheh sharaab meekhorand
rooh kharaab-o mast shod aqhl khomaar meeresad

chon beresee beh-koo-ye maa khaamoshi ast khoo-ye maa
zaan keh ze goftogoo-ye maa gard-o qhobaar meeresad

آب زنید راه را هین که نگار می‌رسد
مژده دهید باغ را بوی بهار می‌رسد

راه دهید یار را آن مه ده چهار را
کز رخ نوربخش او نور نثار می‌رسد

چاک شدست آسمان غلغله‌ایست در جهان
عنبر و مشک می‌دمد سنجق یار می‌رسد

رونق باغ می‌رسد چشم و چراغ می‌رسد
غم به کناره می‌رود مه به کنار می‌رسد

تیر روانه می‌رود سوی نشانه می‌رود
ما چه نشسته‌ایم پس شه ز شکار می‌رسد

باغ سلام می‌کند سرو قیام می‌کند
سبزه پیاده می‌رود غنچه سوار می‌رسد

خلوتیان آسمان تا چه شراب می‌خورند
روح خراب و مست شد عقل خمار می‌رسد

چون برسی به کوی ما خامشی است خوی ما
زآن که ز گفت و گوی ما گرد و غبار می‌رسد

{ 37 }

jam-'e to deedam pas az in heech pareeshaan nashavam
raaH-e to deedam pas as in hamraH-e eeshaan nashavam

ey keh to shaaH-e chamani, seer-kon-e sad cho mani
chashm-o delam seer koni, sokhreh-ye in khaan nashavam

ka'beh cho aamad sooye man, jaaneb-e ka'beh naravam
maaH-e man aamad beh zamin, qhaased-e keyvaan nashavam

farbeH-o por-baad-e to-am, mast-o khosh-o shaad-e to-am
bandeh-vo aazaad-e to-am, bandeh-ye sheytaan nashavam

shaaH-e zameenee-yo zamaan, hamcho kherad faash-o nahaan
peesh-e to ey jaan-o jahaan, jomleh cheraa jaan nashavam?

جمع تو دیدم پس از این هیچ پریشان نشوم
راه تو دیدم پس از این همره ایشان نشوم

ای که تو شاه چمنی سیرکن صد چو منی
چشم و دلم سیر کنی سخرهی این خوان نشوم

کعبه چو آمد سوی من جانب کعبه نروم
ماه من آمد به زمین قاصد کیوان نشوم

فربه و پرباد توام مست و خوش و شاد توام
بنده و آزاد توام بندهی شیطان نشوم

شاه زمینی و زمان همچو خرد فاش و نهان
پیش تو ای جان و جهان جمله چرا جان نشوم

ALSO AVAILABLE:

THE UNIVERSE IN YOU
The first volume in the *Inner Journey* series contains 34 new translations of Rumi, along with the original poems and beautiful illustrations.
ISBN 9780692434451

THE HEART'S GARDEN
Based on a poem by Rumi. This fully illustrated story-book empowers kids and adults by reminding them of their inter-connectedness to all and their ability to transform the world. Winner of the 2015 Gelett Burgess Award.
ISBN 9780692514801

Made in United States
Orlando, FL
18 June 2024

48010287R20087